D1826345

Public Clouds
Complete Self-Assessment Guide

The guidance in this Self-Assessment is based on Public Clouds best practices and standards in business process architecture, design and quality management. The guidance is also based on the professional judgment of the individual collaborators listed in the Acknowledgments.

Notice of rights

Trademarks

Table of Contents

About The Art of Service

The Art of Service, Business Process Architects since 2000, is dedicated to helping stakeholders achieve excellence.

Defining, designing, creating, and implementing a process to solve a stakeholders challenge or meet an objective is the most valuable role... In EVERY group, company, organization and department.

Unless you're talking a one-time, single-use project, there should be a process. Whether that process is managed and implemented by humans, AI, or a combination of the two, it needs to be designed by someone with a complex enough perspective to ask the right questions.

Someone capable of asking the right questions and step back and say, 'What are we really trying to accomplish here? And is there a different way to look at it?'

With The Art of Service's Standard Requirements Self-Assessments, we empower people who can do just that — whether their title is marketer, entrepreneur, manager, salesperson, consultant, Business Process Manager, executive assistant, IT Manager, CIO etc... —they are the people who rule the future. They are people who watch the process as it happens, and ask the right questions to make the process work better.

Contact us when you need any support with this Self-Assessment and any help with templates, blue-prints and examples of standard documents you might need:

http://theartofservice.com
service@theartofservice.com

Included Resources - how to access

Included with your purchase of the book is the Public Clouds

Self-Assessment Spreadsheet Dashboard which contains all questions and Self-Assessment areas and auto-generates insights, graphs, and project RACI planning - all with examples to get you started right away.

How? Simply send an email to
access@theartofservice.com
with this books' title in the subject to get the Public Clouds Self Assessment Tool right away.

You will receive the following contents with New and Updated specific criteria:

• The latest quick edition of the book in PDF

• The latest complete edition of the book in PDF, which criteria correspond to the criteria in...

• The Self-Assessment Excel Dashboard, and...

• Example pre-filled Self-Assessment Excel Dashboard to get familiar with results generation

• In-depth specific Checklists covering the topic

• Project management checklists and templates to assist with implementation

INCLUDES LIFETIME SELF ASSESSMENT UPDATES

Every self assessment comes with Lifetime Updates and Lifetime Free Updated Books. Lifetime Updates is an industry-first feature which allows you to receive verified self assessment updates, ensuring you always have the most accurate information at your fingertips.

Get it now- you will be glad you did - do it now, before you forget.

Send an email to **access@theartofservice.com** with this books' title in the subject to get the Public Clouds Self Assessment Tool right away.

Purpose of this Self-Assessment

This Self-Assessment has been developed to improve understanding of the requirements and elements of Public Clouds, based on best practices and standards in business process architecture, design and quality management.

It is designed to allow for a rapid Self-Assessment to determine how closely existing management practices and procedures correspond to the elements of the Self-Assessment.

The criteria of requirements and elements of Public Clouds have been rephrased in the format of a Self-Assessment questionnaire, with a seven-criterion scoring system, as explained in this document.

In this format, even with limited background knowledge of Public Clouds, a manager can quickly review existing operations to determine how they measure up to the standards. This in turn can serve as the starting point of a 'gap analysis' to identify management tools or system elements that might usefully be implemented in the organization to help improve overall performance.

How to use the Self-Assessment

On the following pages are a series of questions to identify to what extent your Public Clouds initiative is complete in comparison to the requirements set in standards.

To facilitate answering the questions, there is a space in front of each question to enter a score on a scale of '1' to '5'.

1 Strongly Disagree

2 Disagree

3 Neutral

4 Agree

5 Strongly Agree

Read the question and rate it with the following in front of mind:

'In my belief, the answer to this question is clearly defined'.

There are two ways in which you can choose to interpret this statement;
1. how aware are you that the answer to the question is clearly defined
2. for more in-depth analysis you can choose to gather evidence and confirm the answer to the question. This obviously will take more time, most Self-Assessment users opt for the first way to interpret the question and dig deeper later on based on the outcome of the overall Self-Assessment.

A score of '1' would mean that the answer is not clear at all, where a '5' would mean the answer is crystal clear and defined. Leave emtpy when the question is not applicable or you don't want to answer it, you can skip it without affecting your score. Write your score in the space provided.

After you have responded to all the appropriate statements in each section, compute your average score for that section, using the formula provided, and round to the nearest tenth. Then transfer to the corresponding spoke in the Public Clouds Scorecard on the second next page of the Self-Assessment.

Your completed Public Clouds Scorecard will give you a clear presentation of which Public Clouds areas need attention.

Public Clouds
Scorecard Example

Example of how the finalized Scorecard can look like:

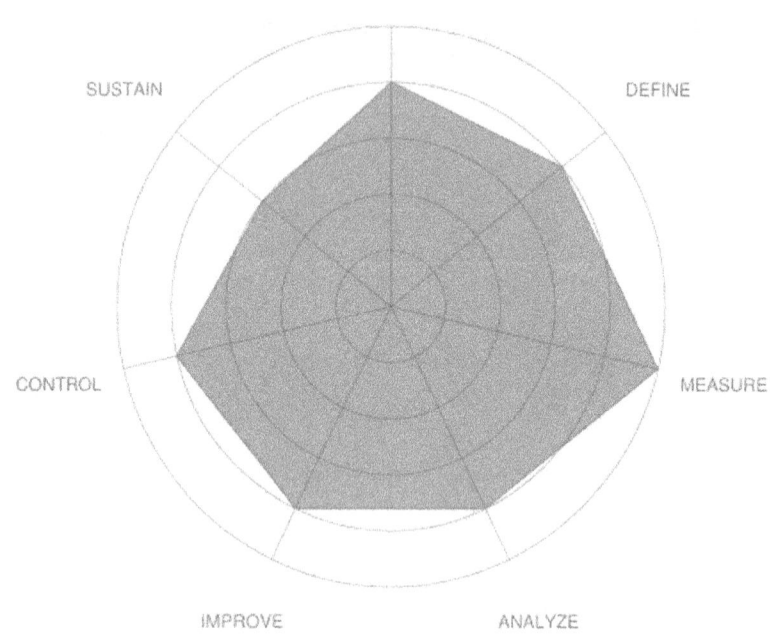

Public Clouds Scorecard

Your Scores:

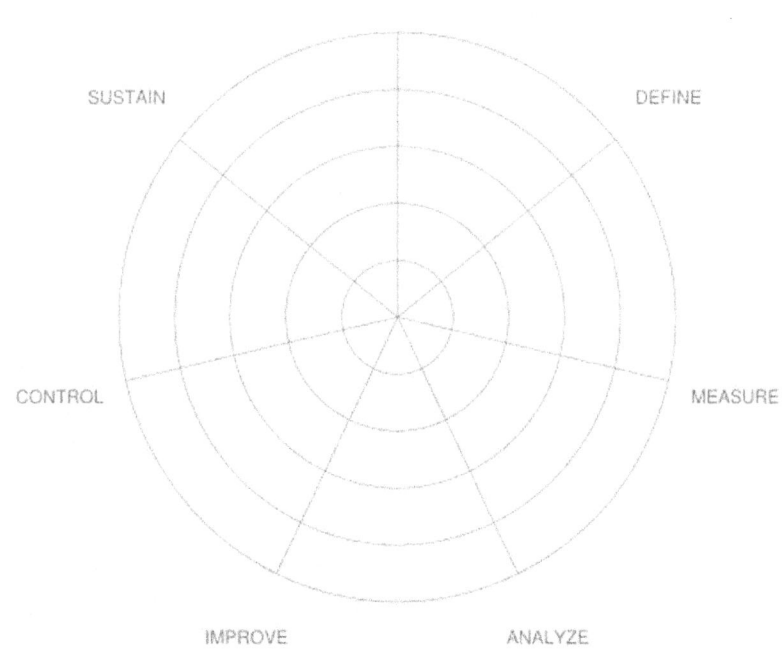

BEGINNING OF THE SELF-ASSESSMENT:

CRITERION #1: RECOGNIZE

INTENT: Be aware of the need for change. Recognize that there is an unfavorable variation, problem or symptom.

In my belief, the answer to this question is clearly defined:

5 Strongly Agree

4 Agree

3 Neutral

2 Disagree

1 Strongly Disagree

1. Are there regulatory / compliance issues?
<--- Score

2. Does your organization need more public clouds education?
<--- Score

3. What creative shifts do you need to take?
<--- Score

4. Who needs to know?
<--- Score

5. What situation(s) led to this public clouds Self Assessment?
<--- Score

6. Where is training needed?
<--- Score

7. What are the public clouds resources needed?
<--- Score

8. What would happen if public clouds weren't done?
<--- Score

9. Who are your key stakeholders who need to sign off?
<--- Score

10. Which needs are not included or involved?
<--- Score

11. Which information does the public clouds business case need to include?
<--- Score

12. For your public clouds project, identify and describe the business environment, is there more than one layer to the business environment?
<--- Score

13. What public clouds problem should be solved?
<--- Score

14. Are there any specific expectations or concerns about the public clouds team, public clouds itself?
<--- Score

15. What is the problem and/or vulnerability?
<--- Score

16. How many trainings, in total, are needed?
<--- Score

17. What extra resources will you need?
<--- Score

18. Did you miss any major public clouds issues?
<--- Score

19. What public clouds capabilities do you need?
<--- Score

20. How are the public clouds's objectives aligned to the group's overall stakeholder strategy?
<--- Score

21. How do you recognize an public clouds objection?
<--- Score

22. Do you need different information or graphics?
<--- Score

23. Are employees recognized or rewarded for performance that demonstrates the highest levels of integrity?
<--- Score

24. What public clouds coordination do you need?
<--- Score

25. What information do users need?
<--- Score

26. What is the public clouds problem definition? What do you need to resolve?
<--- Score

27. What are the expected benefits of public clouds to the stakeholder?
<--- Score

28. Think about the people you identified for your public clouds project and the project responsibilities you would assign to them, what kind of training do you think they would need to perform these responsibilities effectively?
<--- Score

29. How does it fit into your organizational needs and tasks?
<--- Score

30. How do you take a forward-looking perspective in identifying public clouds research related to market response and models?
<--- Score

31. Consider your own public clouds project, what types of organizational problems do you think might be causing or affecting your problem, based on the work done so far?
<--- Score

32. What activities does the governance board need to consider?

<--- Score

33. Looking at each person individually – does every one have the qualities which are needed to work in this group?
<--- Score

34. Who needs budgets?
<--- Score

35. What are the clients issues and concerns?
<--- Score

36. Are your goals realistic? Do you need to redefine your problem? Perhaps the problem has changed or maybe you have reached your goal and need to set a new one?
<--- Score

37. Who needs what information?
<--- Score

38. Are losses recognized in a timely manner?
<--- Score

39. Is the quality assurance team identified?
<--- Score

40. To what extent would your organization benefit from being recognized as a award recipient?
<--- Score

41. How do you recognize an objection?
<--- Score

42. Will new equipment/products be required to

facilitate public clouds delivery, for example is new software needed?

<--- Score

43. Do you have/need 24-hour access to key personnel?

<--- Score

44. Whom do you really need or want to serve?

<--- Score

45. Can management personnel recognize the monetary benefit of public clouds?

<--- Score

46. What else needs to be measured?

<--- Score

47. What training and capacity building actions are needed to implement proposed reforms?

<--- Score

48. Who should resolve the public clouds issues?

<--- Score

49. What is the recognized need?

<--- Score

50. To what extent does each concerned units management team recognize public clouds as an effective investment?

<--- Score

51. Do you need to avoid or amend any public clouds activities?

<--- Score

52. Are controls defined to recognize and contain problems?
<--- Score

53. What needs to be done?
<--- Score

54. How are training requirements identified?
<--- Score

55. Would you recognize a threat from the inside?
<--- Score

56. What public clouds events should you attend?
<--- Score

57. How much are sponsors, customers, partners, stakeholders involved in public clouds? In other words, what are the risks, if public clouds does not deliver successfully?
<--- Score

58. Are you dealing with any of the same issues today as yesterday? What can you do about this?
<--- Score

59. Are there public clouds problems defined?
<--- Score

60. Which issues are too important to ignore?
<--- Score

61. What is the extent or complexity of the public clouds problem?
<--- Score

62. As a sponsor, customer or management, how important is it to meet goals, objectives?
<--- Score

63. What resources or support might you need?
<--- Score

64. Will it solve real problems?
<--- Score

65. Does the problem have ethical dimensions?
<--- Score

66. Why is this needed?
<--- Score

67. What tools and technologies are needed for a custom public clouds project?
<--- Score

68. What are your needs in relation to public clouds skills, labor, equipment, and markets?
<--- Score

69. Why the need?
<--- Score

70. What should be considered when identifying available resources, constraints, and deadlines?
<--- Score

71. Who else hopes to benefit from it?
<--- Score

72. How can auditing be a preventative security

measure?

<--- Score

73. What do you need to start doing?

<--- Score

74. Do you know what you need to know about public clouds?

<--- Score

75. Will public clouds deliverables need to be tested and, if so, by whom?

<--- Score

76. What prevents you from making the changes you know will make you a more effective public clouds leader?

<--- Score

77. What vendors make products that address the public clouds needs?

<--- Score

78. How do you identify subcontractor relationships?

<--- Score

79. What are the stakeholder objectives to be achieved with public clouds?

<--- Score

80. Have you identified your public clouds key performance indicators?

<--- Score

81. Who defines the rules in relation to any given issue?

<--- Score

82. What do employees need in the short term?
<--- Score

83. What problems are you facing and how do you consider public clouds will circumvent those obstacles?
<--- Score

84. What needs to stay?
<--- Score

85. Where do you need to exercise leadership?
<--- Score

86. When a public clouds manager recognizes a problem, what options are available?
<--- Score

87. What does public clouds success mean to the stakeholders?
<--- Score

88. Are there recognized public clouds problems?
<--- Score

89. Is the need for organizational change recognized?
<--- Score

90. Are employees recognized for desired behaviors?
<--- Score

91. Is it needed?
<--- Score

92. Is it clear when you think of the day ahead of you what activities and tasks you need to complete?
<--- Score

93. Are there any revenue recognition issues?
<--- Score

94. Who needs to know about public clouds?
<--- Score

95. How are you going to measure success?
<--- Score

96. What are the minority interests and what amount of minority interests can be recognized?
<--- Score

97. What are the timeframes required to resolve each of the issues/problems?
<--- Score

98. Does public clouds create potential expectations in other areas that need to be recognized and considered?
<--- Score

Add up total points for this section:
_____ = Total points for this section

Divided by: _____ (number of statements answered) = _____
Average score for this section

Transfer your score to the public clouds Index at the beginning of the Self-Assessment.

CRITERION #2: DEFINE:

INTENT: Formulate the stakeholder problem. Define the problem, needs and objectives.

In my belief, the answer to this question is clearly defined:

5 Strongly Agree

4 Agree

3 Neutral

2 Disagree

1 Strongly Disagree

1. Has a team charter been developed and communicated?
<--- Score

2. Are there different segments of customers?
<--- Score

3. Do the problem and goal statements meet the SMART criteria (specific, measurable, attainable,

relevant, and time-bound)?
<--- Score

4. What are the Roles and Responsibilities for each team member and its leadership? Where is this documented?
<--- Score

5. What is the scope of the public clouds effort?
<--- Score

6. Is there any additional public clouds definition of success?
<--- Score

7. What public clouds requirements should be gathered?
<--- Score

8. Have all of the relationships been defined properly?
<--- Score

9. How and when will the baselines be defined?
<--- Score

10. Will team members perform public clouds work when assigned and in a timely fashion?
<--- Score

11. Is the public clouds scope complete and appropriately sized?
<--- Score

12. Is it clearly defined in and to your organization what you do?
<--- Score

13. Is the public clouds scope manageable?
<--- Score

14. Is there a completed SIPOC representation, describing the Suppliers, Inputs, Process, Outputs, and Customers?
<--- Score

15. How do you gather requirements?
<--- Score

16. How will the public clouds team and the group measure complete success of public clouds?
<--- Score

17. Has the improvement team collected the 'voice of the customer' (obtained feedback – qualitative and quantitative)?
<--- Score

18. What would be the goal or target for a public clouds's improvement team?
<--- Score

19. Who is gathering public clouds information?
<--- Score

20. Is public clouds required?
<--- Score

21. What information do you gather?
<--- Score

22. Is the current 'as is' process being followed? If not, what are the discrepancies?

<--- Score

23. Are resources adequate for the scope?
<--- Score

24. Why are you doing public clouds and what is the scope?
<--- Score

25. What are (control) requirements for public clouds Information?
<--- Score

26. What happens if public clouds's scope changes?
<--- Score

27. Has a high-level 'as is' process map been completed, verified and validated?
<--- Score

28. Will team members regularly document their public clouds work?
<--- Score

29. Are required metrics defined, what are they?
<--- Score

30. How can the value of public clouds be defined?
<--- Score

31. Are the public clouds requirements testable?
<--- Score

32. Are approval levels defined for contracts and supplements to contracts?
<--- Score

33. Who is gathering information?
<--- Score

34. Do you have a public clouds success story or case study ready to tell and share?
<--- Score

35. What baselines are required to be defined and managed?
<--- Score

36. What knowledge or experience is required?
<--- Score

37. Has the direction changed at all during the course of public clouds? If so, when did it change and why?
<--- Score

38. Will a public clouds production readiness review be required?
<--- Score

39. How will variation in the actual durations of each activity be dealt with to ensure that the expected public clouds results are met?
<--- Score

40. Is the scope of public clouds defined?
<--- Score

41. Is special public clouds user knowledge required?
<--- Score

42. Have specific policy objectives been defined?
<--- Score

43. Are all requirements met?
<--- Score

44. What sources do you use to gather information for a public clouds study?
<--- Score

45. How do you keep key subject matter experts in the loop?
<--- Score

46. When is the estimated completion date?
<--- Score

47. What information should you gather?
<--- Score

48. How do you think the partners involved in public clouds would have defined success?
<--- Score

49. Is there a clear public clouds case definition?
<--- Score

50. What are the record-keeping requirements of public clouds activities?
<--- Score

51. When is/was the public clouds start date?
<--- Score

52. Has your scope been defined?
<--- Score

53. What are the compelling stakeholder reasons for

embarking on public clouds?
<--- Score

54. How do you hand over public clouds context?
<--- Score

55. Is there a critical path to deliver public clouds results?
<--- Score

56. What sort of initial information to gather?
<--- Score

57. What specifically is the problem? Where does it occur? When does it occur? What is its extent?
<--- Score

58. Are there any constraints known that bear on the ability to perform public clouds work? How is the team addressing them?
<--- Score

59. What customer feedback methods were used to solicit their input?
<--- Score

60. How do you gather the stories?
<--- Score

61. Is there regularly 100% attendance at the team meetings? If not, have appointed substitutes attended to preserve cross-functionality and full representation?
<--- Score

62. How do you catch public clouds definition

inconsistencies?
<--- Score

63. How have you defined all public clouds requirements first?
<--- Score

64. Has everyone on the team, including the team leaders, been properly trained?
<--- Score

65. How did the public clouds manager receive input to the development of a public clouds improvement plan and the estimated completion dates/times of each activity?
<--- Score

66. What are the rough order estimates on cost savings/opportunities that public clouds brings?
<--- Score

67. How often are the team meetings?
<--- Score

68. Who defines (or who defined) the rules and roles?
<--- Score

69. What is out of scope?
<--- Score

70. What are the boundaries of the scope? What is in bounds and what is not? What is the start point? What is the stop point?
<--- Score

71. What is in the scope and what is not in scope?

<--- Score

72. Have all basic functions of public clouds been defined?
<--- Score

73. What is in scope?
<--- Score

74. Is there a completed, verified, and validated high-level 'as is' (not 'should be' or 'could be') stakeholder process map?
<--- Score

75. Who are the public clouds improvement team members, including Management Leads and Coaches?
<--- Score

76. What defines best in class?
<--- Score

77. What is the definition of public clouds excellence?
<--- Score

78. Is the improvement team aware of the different versions of a process: what they think it is vs. what it actually is vs. what it should be vs. what it could be?
<--- Score

79. Has the public clouds work been fairly and/ or equitably divided and delegated among team members who are qualified and capable to perform the work? Has everyone contributed?
<--- Score

80. How was the 'as is' process map developed, reviewed, verified and validated?
<--- Score

81. What is the definition of success?
<--- Score

82. Are accountability and ownership for public clouds clearly defined?
<--- Score

83. Scope of sensitive information?
<--- Score

84. Is full participation by members in regularly held team meetings guaranteed?
<--- Score

85. How do you gather public clouds requirements?
<--- Score

86. Is the team equipped with available and reliable resources?
<--- Score

87. What constraints exist that might impact the team?
<--- Score

88. Is scope creep really all bad news?
<--- Score

89. What critical content must be communicated – who, what, when, where, and how?
<--- Score

90. The political context: who holds power?
<--- Score

91. Are different versions of process maps needed to account for the different types of inputs?
<--- Score

92. What are the dynamics of the communication plan?
<--- Score

93. What are the requirements for audit information?
<--- Score

94. How do you manage unclear public clouds requirements?
<--- Score

95. How is the team tracking and documenting its work?
<--- Score

96. In the case of public clouds, will the hosting service provider meet regulatory compliance requirements?
<--- Score

97. In what way can you redefine the criteria of choice clients have in your category in your favor?
<--- Score

98. What system do you use for gathering public clouds information?
<--- Score

99. Who approved the public clouds scope?

<--- Score

100. How does the public clouds manager ensure against scope creep?
<--- Score

101. How do you manage changes in public clouds requirements?
<--- Score

102. Are task requirements clearly defined?
<--- Score

103. What is the scope of the public clouds work?
<--- Score

104. What is the scope of public clouds?
<--- Score

105. Are customer(s) identified and segmented according to their different needs and requirements?
<--- Score

106. What are the public clouds use cases?
<--- Score

107. Does the team have regular meetings?
<--- Score

108. What is a worst-case scenario for losses?
<--- Score

109. What scope do you want your strategy to cover?
<--- Score

110. Has anyone else (internal or external to the

group) attempted to solve this problem or a similar one before? If so, what knowledge can be leveraged from these previous efforts?
<--- Score

111. What scope to assess?
<--- Score

112. When are meeting minutes sent out? Who is on the distribution list?
<--- Score

113. What gets examined?
<--- Score

114. Where can you gather more information?
<--- Score

115. Are roles and responsibilities formally defined?
<--- Score

116. Are the public clouds requirements complete?
<--- Score

117. Is public clouds currently on schedule according to the plan?
<--- Score

118. What key stakeholder process output measure(s) does public clouds leverage and how?
<--- Score

119. Are audit criteria, scope, frequency and methods defined?
<--- Score

120. What is out-of-scope initially?
<--- Score

121. Do you have organizational privacy requirements?
<--- Score

122. What intelligence can you gather?
<--- Score

123. If substitutes have been appointed, have they been briefed on the public clouds goals and received regular communications as to the progress to date?
<--- Score

124. What are the tasks and definitions?
<--- Score

125. What are the public clouds tasks and definitions?
<--- Score

126. Is the team adequately staffed with the desired cross-functionality? If not, what additional resources are available to the team?
<--- Score

127. Has a project plan, Gantt chart, or similar been developed/completed?
<--- Score

128. Is the work to date meeting requirements?
<--- Score

129. How are consistent public clouds definitions important?
<--- Score

130. Is public clouds linked to key stakeholder goals and objectives?
<--- Score

131. Have the customer needs been translated into specific, measurable requirements? How?
<--- Score

132. What was the context?
<--- Score

133. How would you define public clouds leadership?
<--- Score

134. What public clouds services do you require?
<--- Score

135. How do you build the right business case?
<--- Score

136. Has/have the customer(s) been identified?
<--- Score

137. Is data collected and displayed to better understand customer(s) critical needs and requirements.
<--- Score

138. How would you define the culture at your organization, how susceptible is it to public clouds changes?
<--- Score

139. Is there a public clouds management charter, including stakeholder case, problem and

goal statements, scope, milestones, roles and
responsibilities, communication plan?
<--- Score

Add up total points for this section:
_ _ _ _ _ = Total points for this section

Divided by: _ _ _ _ _ _ (number of
statements answered) = _ _ _ _ _ _
Average score for this section

Transfer your score to the public clouds
Index at the beginning of the Self-
Assessment.

CRITERION #3: MEASURE:

INTENT: Gather the correct data.
Measure the current performance and
evolution of the situation.

In my belief, the answer to this
question is clearly defined:

5 Strongly Agree

4 Agree

3 Neutral

2 Disagree

1 Strongly Disagree

1. Among the public clouds product and service
cost to be estimated, which is considered hardest to
estimate?
<--- Score

2. Are there competing public clouds priorities?
<--- Score

3. Are there measurements based on task

performance?
<--- Score

4. When a disaster occurs, who gets priority?
<--- Score

5. What methods are feasible and acceptable to estimate the impact of reforms?
<--- Score

6. How is progress measured?
<--- Score

7. How will you measure success?
<--- Score

8. Are you able to realize any cost savings?
<--- Score

9. What does a Test Case verify?
<--- Score

10. How are measurements made?
<--- Score

11. How do you measure lifecycle phases?
<--- Score

12. What is the cost of rework?
<--- Score

13. What are the costs?
<--- Score

14. How do you quantify and qualify impacts?
<--- Score

15. What evidence is there and what is measured?
<--- Score

16. How do you measure variability?
<--- Score

17. Are indirect costs charged to the public clouds program?
<--- Score

18. How much does it cost?
<--- Score

19. How will success or failure be measured?
<--- Score

20. Do you aggressively reward and promote the people who have the biggest impact on creating excellent public clouds services/products?
<--- Score

21. What are the public clouds key cost drivers?
<--- Score

22. Where is the cost?
<--- Score

23. What are the types and number of measures to use?
<--- Score

24. Are there any easy-to-implement alternatives to public clouds? Sometimes other solutions are available that do not require the cost implications of a full-blown project?

<--- Score

25. What are your primary costs, revenues, assets?
<--- Score

26. What could cause you to change course?
<--- Score

27. What are the public clouds investment costs?
<--- Score

28. What is your decision requirements diagram?
<--- Score

29. What causes innovation to fail or succeed in your organization?
<--- Score

30. What drives O&M cost?
<--- Score

31. What are you verifying?
<--- Score

32. How do your measurements capture actionable public clouds information for use in exceeding your customers expectations and securing your customers engagement?
<--- Score

33. When are costs are incurred?
<--- Score

34. Do you effectively measure and reward individual and team performance?
<--- Score

35. How can you reduce the costs of obtaining inputs?
<--- Score

36. How can you measure the performance?
<--- Score

37. What is the cause of any public clouds gaps?
<--- Score

38. Do you have a flow diagram of what happens?
<--- Score

39. Does management have the right priorities among projects?
<--- Score

40. How can you measure public clouds in a systematic way?
<--- Score

41. Are the units of measure consistent?
<--- Score

42. How will measures be used to manage and adapt?
<--- Score

43. Why do you expend time and effort to implement measurement, for whom?
<--- Score

44. At what cost?
<--- Score

45. What potential environmental factors impact the public clouds effort?

<--- Score

46. How do you verify and validate the public clouds data?
<--- Score

47. What is the total cost related to deploying public clouds, including any consulting or professional services?
<--- Score

48. What causes extra work or rework?
<--- Score

49. What is the total fixed cost?
<--- Score

50. Are you aware of what could cause a problem?
<--- Score

51. Are actual costs in line with budgeted costs?
<--- Score

52. What are the uncertainties surrounding estimates of impact?
<--- Score

53. What are your operating costs?
<--- Score

54. How do you verify the authenticity of the data and information used?
<--- Score

55. What does your operating model cost?
<--- Score

56. Does the public clouds task fit the client's priorities?
<--- Score

57. Which costs should be taken into account?
<--- Score

58. What are the current costs of the public clouds process?
<--- Score

59. What details are required of the public clouds cost structure?
<--- Score

60. What are the costs of delaying public clouds action?
<--- Score

61. What can be used to verify compliance?
<--- Score

62. When should you bother with diagrams?
<--- Score

63. Does a public clouds quantification method exist?
<--- Score

64. Are missed public clouds opportunities costing your organization money?
<--- Score

65. Who pays the cost?
<--- Score

66. What would be a real cause for concern?
<--- Score

67. Is the solution cost-effective?
<--- Score

68. Which public clouds impacts are significant?
<--- Score

69. Are supply costs steady or fluctuating?
<--- Score

70. Which measures and indicators matter?
<--- Score

71. How are costs allocated?
<--- Score

72. How to cause the change?
<--- Score

73. Have you included everything in your public clouds cost models?
<--- Score

74. What users will be impacted?
<--- Score

75. How do you measure success?
<--- Score

76. What are allowable costs?
<--- Score

77. Will public clouds have an impact on current business continuity, disaster recovery processes and/

or infrastructure?
<--- Score

78. How frequently do you track public clouds measures?
<--- Score

79. What would it cost to replace your technology?
<--- Score

80. What tests verify requirements?
<--- Score

81. What is an unallowable cost?
<--- Score

82. What are hidden public clouds quality costs?
<--- Score

83. Do you have an issue in getting priority?
<--- Score

84. How do you verify if public clouds is built right?
<--- Score

85. How do you control the overall costs of your work processes?
<--- Score

86. Do you have any cost public clouds limitation requirements?
<--- Score

87. Where is it measured?
<--- Score

88. How do you aggregate measures across priorities?
<--- Score

89. Are public clouds vulnerabilities categorized and prioritized?
<--- Score

90. How will costs be allocated?
<--- Score

91. Who should receive measurement reports?
<--- Score

92. What are the costs and benefits?
<--- Score

93. How will your organization measure success?
<--- Score

94. Has a cost center been established?
<--- Score

95. Is there an opportunity to verify requirements?
<--- Score

96. How do you measure efficient delivery of public clouds services?
<--- Score

97. How can you reduce costs?
<--- Score

98. What are the strategic priorities for this year?
<--- Score

99. What measurements are being captured?

<--- Score

100. Are the measurements objective?
<--- Score

101. Is the cost worth the public clouds effort ?
<--- Score

102. How can you manage cost down?
<--- Score

103. How will you measure your public clouds effectiveness?
<--- Score

104. What is the root cause(s) of the problem?
<--- Score

105. How do you verify the public clouds requirements quality?
<--- Score

106. How is the value delivered by public clouds being measured?
<--- Score

107. Are the public clouds benefits worth its costs?
<--- Score

108. What do people want to verify?
<--- Score

109. What could cause delays in the schedule?
<--- Score

110. How do you verify and develop ideas and

innovations?
<--- Score

111. How sensitive must the public clouds strategy be to cost?
<--- Score

112. What are your key public clouds organizational performance measures, including key short and longer-term financial measures?
<--- Score

113. Was a business case (cost/benefit) developed?
<--- Score

114. Have you made assumptions about the shape of the future, particularly its impact on your customers and competitors?
<--- Score

115. What is the public clouds business impact?
<--- Score

116. What do you measure and why?
<--- Score

117. Do the benefits outweigh the costs?
<--- Score

118. What are your customers expectations and measures?
<--- Score

119. What causes investor action?
<--- Score

120. What is your public clouds quality cost segregation study?
<--- Score

121. How long to keep data and how to manage retention costs?
<--- Score

122. Why do the measurements/indicators matter?
<--- Score

123. What are the operational costs after public clouds deployment?
<--- Score

124. How do you verify your resources?
<--- Score

125. Did you tackle the cause or the symptom?
<--- Score

126. What disadvantage does this cause for the user?
<--- Score

127. What measurements are possible, practicable and meaningful?
<--- Score

128. How will effects be measured?
<--- Score

129. How do you verify performance?
<--- Score

130. What are the costs of reform?
<--- Score

131. Are you taking your company in the direction of better and revenue or cheaper and cost?
<--- Score

132. What does losing customers cost your organization?
<--- Score

133. What is measured? Why?
<--- Score

Add up total points for this section:
_____ = Total points for this section

Divided by: _____ (number of statements answered) = _____
Average score for this section

Transfer your score to the public clouds Index at the beginning of the Self-Assessment.

CRITERION #4: ANALYZE:

INTENT: Analyze causes, assumptions and hypotheses.

In my belief, the answer to this question is clearly defined:

5 Strongly Agree

4 Agree

3 Neutral

2 Disagree

1 Strongly Disagree

1. What process improvements will be needed?
<--- Score

2. How do you identify specific public clouds investment opportunities and emerging trends?
<--- Score

3. How is the data gathered?
<--- Score

4. What does the data say about the performance of the stakeholder process?
<--- Score

5. What are your outputs?
<--- Score

6. How do you implement and manage your work processes to ensure that they meet design requirements?
<--- Score

7. Do you, as a leader, bounce back quickly from setbacks?
<--- Score

8. What is your organizations system for selecting qualified vendors?
<--- Score

9. Are you missing public clouds opportunities?
<--- Score

10. How do you use public clouds data and information to support organizational decision making and innovation?
<--- Score

11. Should you invest in industry-recognized qualifications?
<--- Score

12. Is the final output clearly identified?
<--- Score

13. How are outputs preserved and protected?

<--- Score

14. Has data output been validated?
<--- Score

15. Do several people in different organizational units assist with the public clouds process?
<--- Score

16. Is there any way to speed up the process?
<--- Score

17. How will the public clouds data be captured?
<--- Score

18. Where is public clouds data gathered?
<--- Score

19. What public clouds data will be collected?
<--- Score

20. How difficult is it to qualify what public clouds ROI is?
<--- Score

21. What information qualified as important?
<--- Score

22. What systems/processes must you excel at?
<--- Score

23. How is the public clouds Value Stream Mapping managed?
<--- Score

24. Who owns what data?

<--- Score

25. How do you promote understanding that opportunity for improvement is not criticism of the status quo, or the people who created the status quo?
<--- Score

26. What, related to, public clouds processes does your organization outsource?
<--- Score

27. How do you ensure that the public clouds opportunity is realistic?
<--- Score

28. What is the output?
<--- Score

29. Are all team members qualified for all tasks?
<--- Score

30. What other jobs or tasks affect the performance of the steps in the public clouds process?
<--- Score

31. What were the financial benefits resulting from any 'ground fruit or low-hanging fruit' (quick fixes)?
<--- Score

32. Which public clouds data should be retained?
<--- Score

33. What quality tools were used to get through the analyze phase?
<--- Score

34. Is there a strict change management process?
<--- Score

35. What are the disruptive public clouds technologies that enable your organization to radically change your business processes?
<--- Score

36. Is the gap/opportunity displayed and communicated in financial terms?
<--- Score

37. What are your current levels and trends in key measures or indicators of public clouds product and process performance that are important to and directly serve your customers? How do these results compare with the performance of your competitors and other organizations with similar offerings?
<--- Score

38. A compounding model resolution with available relevant data can often provide insight towards a solution methodology; which public clouds models, tools and techniques are necessary?
<--- Score

39. What is the oversight process?
<--- Score

40. What conclusions were drawn from the team's data collection and analysis? How did the team reach these conclusions?
<--- Score

41. What data is gathered?
<--- Score

42. Are public clouds changes recognized early enough to be approved through the regular process?
<--- Score

43. How do you measure the operational performance of your key work systems and processes, including productivity, cycle time, and other appropriate measures of process effectiveness, efficiency, and innovation?
<--- Score

44. How will the data be checked for quality?
<--- Score

45. Is the suppliers process defined and controlled?
<--- Score

46. Record-keeping requirements flow from the records needed as inputs, outputs, controls and for transformation of a public clouds process, are the records needed as inputs to the public clouds process available?
<--- Score

47. Do your employees have the opportunity to do what they do best everyday?
<--- Score

48. What kind of crime could a potential new hire have committed that would not only not disqualify him/her from being hired by your organization, but would actually indicate that he/she might be a particularly good fit?
<--- Score

49. How often will data be collected for measures?
<--- Score

50. Have any additional benefits been identified that will result from closing all or most of the gaps?
<--- Score

51. How does the organization define, manage, and improve its public clouds processes?
<--- Score

52. What are evaluation criteria for the output?
<--- Score

53. What process should you select for improvement?
<--- Score

54. How do your work systems and key work processes relate to and capitalize on your core competencies?
<--- Score

55. Were there any improvement opportunities identified from the process analysis?
<--- Score

56. Think about some of the processes you undertake within your organization, which do you own?
<--- Score

57. Who gets your output?
<--- Score

58. What resources go in to get the desired output?
<--- Score

59. What are the public clouds business drivers?
<--- Score

60. What qualifies as competition?
<--- Score

61. What are your key performance measures or indicators and in-process measures for the control and improvement of your public clouds processes?
<--- Score

62. Think about the functions involved in your public clouds project, what processes flow from these functions?
<--- Score

63. How is data used for program management and improvement?
<--- Score

64. Can you add value to the current public clouds decision-making process (largely qualitative) by incorporating uncertainty modeling (more quantitative)?
<--- Score

65. What is the right advice to give business partners and customers when it comes to private clouds, public clouds, data security in the cloud or storage?
<--- Score

66. Is there an established change management process?
<--- Score

67. What training and qualifications will you need?
<--- Score

68. Have the problem and goal statements been updated to reflect the additional knowledge gained from the analyze phase?
<--- Score

69. When should a process be art not science?
<--- Score

70. Has an output goal been set?
<--- Score

71. Where is the data coming from to measure compliance?
<--- Score

72. Were Pareto charts (or similar) used to portray the 'heavy hitters' (or key sources of variation)?
<--- Score

73. Who is involved in the management review process?
<--- Score

74. Do your leaders quickly bounce back from setbacks?
<--- Score

75. Do your contracts/agreements contain data security obligations?
<--- Score

76. What tools were used to generate the list of possible causes?

<--- Score

77. What public clouds data should be collected?
<--- Score

78. Who will facilitate the team and process?
<--- Score

79. How was the detailed process map generated, verified, and validated?
<--- Score

80. Is the required public clouds data gathered?
<--- Score

81. How many input/output points does it require?
<--- Score

82. What controls do you have in place to protect data?
<--- Score

83. What are your best practices for minimizing public clouds project risk, while demonstrating incremental value and quick wins throughout the public clouds project lifecycle?
<--- Score

84. Do staff qualifications match your project?
<--- Score

85. Is the public clouds process severely broken such that a re-design is necessary?
<--- Score

86. How will the change process be managed?

<--- Score

87. What public clouds data do you gather or use now?
<--- Score

88. How will corresponding data be collected?
<--- Score

89. What data do you need to collect?
<--- Score

90. How much data can be collected in the given timeframe?
<--- Score

91. Who is involved with workflow mapping?
<--- Score

92. Are your outputs consistent?
<--- Score

93. Are all staff in core public clouds subjects Highly Qualified?
<--- Score

94. What qualifications do public clouds leaders need?
<--- Score

95. Is the performance gap determined?
<--- Score

96. What is the Value Stream Mapping?
<--- Score

97. What public clouds data should be managed?

<--- Score

98. Identify an operational issue in your organization, for example, could a particular task be done more quickly or more efficiently by public clouds?
<--- Score

99. What were the crucial 'moments of truth' on the process map?
<--- Score

100. What public clouds metrics are outputs of the process?
<--- Score

101. Were any designed experiments used to generate additional insight into the data analysis?
<--- Score

102. What will drive public clouds change?
<--- Score

103. What are the processes for audit reporting and management?
<--- Score

104. How has the public clouds data been gathered?
<--- Score

105. What types of data do your public clouds indicators require?
<--- Score

106. An organizationally feasible system request is one that considers the mission, goals and objectives of the organization, key questions are: is the public

clouds solution request practical and will it solve
a problem or take advantage of an opportunity to
achieve company goals?
<--- Score

107. What are the personnel training and
qualifications required?
<--- Score

108. How do you define collaboration and team
output?
<--- Score

109. Was a cause-and-effect diagram used to explore
the different types of causes (or sources of variation)?
<--- Score

110. How can risk management be tied procedurally
to process elements?
<--- Score

111. What are your public clouds processes?
<--- Score

112. What tools were used to narrow the list of
possible causes?
<--- Score

113. What output to create?
<--- Score

114. Is data and process analysis, root cause analysis
and quantifying the gap/opportunity in place?
<--- Score

115. Was a detailed process map created to amplify

critical steps of the 'as is' stakeholder process?

<--- Score

116. What can you do to prevent data loss in public clouds?

<--- Score

117. What are the public clouds design outputs?

<--- Score

118. What is the public clouds Driver?

<--- Score

119. Do you understand your management processes today?

<--- Score

120. What are your current levels and trends in key public clouds measures or indicators of product and process performance that are important to and directly serve your customers?

<--- Score

121. What is your organizations process which leads to recognition of value generation?

<--- Score

122. Where can you get qualified talent today?

<--- Score

123. What is the complexity of the output produced?

<--- Score

124. What are the best opportunities for value improvement?

<--- Score

125. What successful thing are you doing today that may be blinding you to new growth opportunities?
<--- Score

126. Is pre-qualification of suppliers carried out?
<--- Score

127. What methods do you use to gather public clouds data?
<--- Score

128. How is public clouds data gathered?
<--- Score

129. Have you defined which data is gathered how?
<--- Score

130. What are the revised rough estimates of the financial savings/opportunity for public clouds improvements?
<--- Score

131. What did the team gain from developing a sub-process map?
<--- Score

132. What other organizational variables, such as reward systems or communication systems, affect the performance of this public clouds process?
<--- Score

133. Do you have the authority to produce the output?
<--- Score

134. What is the cost of poor quality as supported by the team's analysis?
<--- Score

Add up total points for this section:
_____ = Total points for this section

Divided by: _____ (number of statements answered) = _____
Average score for this section

Transfer your score to the public clouds Index at the beginning of the Self-Assessment.

CRITERION #5: IMPROVE:

INTENT: Develop a practical solution.
Innovate, establish and test the
solution and to measure the results.

In my belief, the answer to this
question is clearly defined:

5 Strongly Agree

4 Agree

3 Neutral

2 Disagree

1 Strongly Disagree

1. What are the expected public clouds results?
<--- Score

2. What is the implementation plan?
<--- Score

3. Is any public clouds documentation required?
<--- Score

4. How risky is your organization?
<--- Score

5. How do you manage public clouds risk?
<--- Score

6. Risk factors: what are the characteristics of public clouds that make it risky?
<--- Score

7. How can you improve performance?
<--- Score

8. What actually has to improve and by how much?
<--- Score

9. What current systems have to be understood and/or changed?
<--- Score

10. Does the goal represent a desired result that can be measured?
<--- Score

11. What is the risk?
<--- Score

12. What does the 'should be' process map/design look like?
<--- Score

13. Is there a high likelihood that any recommendations will achieve their intended results?
<--- Score

14. How can skill-level changes improve public

clouds?
<--- Score

15. Who controls key decisions that will be made?
<--- Score

16. Who are the people involved in developing and implementing public clouds?
<--- Score

17. Who will be using the results of the measurement activities?
<--- Score

18. How do you define the solutions' scope?
<--- Score

19. What can you do to improve?
<--- Score

20. Are the risks fully understood, reasonable and manageable?
<--- Score

21. How do you improve your likelihood of success ?
<--- Score

22. How do you link measurement and risk?
<--- Score

23. What tools were used to tap into the creativity and encourage 'outside the box' thinking?
<--- Score

24. What went well, what should change, what can improve?

<--- Score

25. Are the most efficient solutions problem-specific?
<--- Score

26. How do you manage and improve your public clouds work systems to deliver customer value and achieve organizational success and sustainability?
<--- Score

27. How is continuous improvement applied to risk management?
<--- Score

28. Where do you need public clouds improvement?
<--- Score

29. How does the team improve its work?
<--- Score

30. What do you want to improve?
<--- Score

31. How will you measure the results?
<--- Score

32. Who manages supplier risk management in your organization?
<--- Score

33. Is there any other public clouds solution?
<--- Score

34. To what extent does management recognize public clouds as a tool to increase the results?
<--- Score

35. Is supporting public clouds documentation required?
<--- Score

36. Do you need to do a usability evaluation?
<--- Score

37. How can the phases of public clouds development be identified?
<--- Score

38. Is risk periodically assessed?
<--- Score

39. What is the public clouds's sustainability risk?
<--- Score

40. Was a public clouds charter developed?
<--- Score

41. How do the public clouds results compare with the performance of your competitors and other organizations with similar offerings?
<--- Score

42. Is the public clouds risk managed?
<--- Score

43. What area needs the greatest improvement?
<--- Score

44. Who are the key stakeholders for the public clouds evaluation?
<--- Score

45. What criteria will you use to assess your public clouds risks?
<--- Score

46. What improvements have been achieved?
<--- Score

47. What alternative responses are available to manage risk?
<--- Score

48. If you could go back in time five years, what decision would you make differently? What is your best guess as to what decision you're making today you might regret five years from now?
<--- Score

49. Are you assessing public clouds and risk?
<--- Score

50. Who do you report public clouds results to?
<--- Score

51. What is the team's contingency plan for potential problems occurring in implementation?
<--- Score

52. Is the solution technically practical?
<--- Score

53. Do vendor agreements bring new compliance risk ?
<--- Score

54. What should a proof of concept or pilot accomplish?

<--- Score

55. What tools were used to evaluate the potential solutions?
<--- Score

56. Does a good decision guarantee a good outcome?
<--- Score

57. What lessons, if any, from a pilot were incorporated into the design of the full-scale solution?
<--- Score

58. Can you identify any significant risks or exposures to public clouds third- parties (vendors, service providers, alliance partners etc) that concern you?
<--- Score

59. How do you improve productivity?
<--- Score

60. Who will be responsible for making the decisions to include or exclude requested changes once public clouds is underway?
<--- Score

61. Is the public clouds documentation thorough?
<--- Score

62. Who manages public clouds risk?
<--- Score

63. How do you measure improved public clouds service perception, and satisfaction?
<--- Score

64. Where do the public clouds decisions reside?
<--- Score

65. How will you recognize and celebrate results?
<--- Score

66. Are risk triggers captured?
<--- Score

67. How do you decide how much to remunerate an employee?
<--- Score

68. Why improve in the first place?
<--- Score

69. Who will be responsible for documenting the public clouds requirements in detail?
<--- Score

70. Who controls the risk?
<--- Score

71. What error proofing will be done to address some of the discrepancies observed in the 'as is' process?
<--- Score

72. Are decisions made in a timely manner?
<--- Score

73. What practices helps your organization to develop its capacity to recognize patterns?
<--- Score

74. Who makes the public clouds decisions in your organization?

<--- Score

75. Have you achieved public clouds improvements?
<--- Score

76. Is the measure of success for public clouds understandable to a variety of people?
<--- Score

77. How do you measure progress and evaluate training effectiveness?
<--- Score

78. What to do with the results or outcomes of measurements?
<--- Score

79. How do you measure risk?
<--- Score

80. What resources are required for the improvement efforts?
<--- Score

81. What public clouds improvements can be made?
<--- Score

82. Are risk management tasks balanced centrally and locally?
<--- Score

83. Do you cover the five essential competencies: Communication, Collaboration,Innovation, Adaptability, and Leadership that improve an organizations ability to leverage the new public clouds in a volatile global economy?

<--- Score

84. How do you improve public clouds service perception, and satisfaction?
<--- Score

85. public clouds risk decisions: whose call Is It?
<--- Score

86. Who are the public clouds decision-makers?
<--- Score

87. How do you keep improving public clouds?
<--- Score

88. How will you know that a change is an improvement?
<--- Score

89. Are the key business and technology risks being managed?
<--- Score

90. How will you know when its improved?
<--- Score

91. What were the underlying assumptions on the cost-benefit analysis?
<--- Score

92. What risks do you need to manage?
<--- Score

93. Who are the public clouds decision makers?
<--- Score

94. What are the public clouds security risks?
<--- Score

95. How will you know that you have improved?
<--- Score

96. Do you have the optimal project management team structure?
<--- Score

97. What are the concrete public clouds results?
<--- Score

98. What is public clouds's impact on utilizing the best solution(s)?
<--- Score

99. Is public clouds documentation maintained?
<--- Score

100. How are policy decisions made and where?
<--- Score

101. At what point will vulnerability assessments be performed once public clouds is put into production (e.g., ongoing Risk Management after implementation)?
<--- Score

102. Are events managed to resolution?
<--- Score

103. Which of the recognised risks out of all risks can be most likely transferred?
<--- Score

104. What were the criteria for evaluating a public clouds pilot?
<--- Score

105. Which public clouds solution is appropriate?
<--- Score

106. What tools were most useful during the improve phase?
<--- Score

107. For estimation problems, how do you develop an estimation statement?
<--- Score

108. Will the controls trigger any other risks?
<--- Score

109. In the past few months, what is the smallest change you have made that has had the biggest positive result? What was it about that small change that produced the large return?
<--- Score

110. Have you identified breakpoints and/or risk tolerances that will trigger broad consideration of a potential need for intervention or modification of strategy?
<--- Score

111. Do those selected for the public clouds team have a good general understanding of what public clouds is all about?
<--- Score

112. Can the solution be designed and implemented

within an acceptable time period?
<--- Score

113. Is the scope clearly documented?
<--- Score

114. What tools do you use once you have decided on a public clouds strategy and more importantly how do you choose?
<--- Score

115. Are procedures documented for managing public clouds risks?
<--- Score

116. What are the implications of the one critical public clouds decision 10 minutes, 10 months, and 10 years from now?
<--- Score

117. Who should make the public clouds decisions?
<--- Score

118. When you map the key players in your own work and the types/domains of relationships with them, which relationships do you find easy and which challenging, and why?
<--- Score

119. Can you integrate quality management and risk management?
<--- Score

120. What needs improvement? Why?
<--- Score

121. Is the public clouds solution sustainable?
<--- Score

122. How can you better manage risk?
<--- Score

123. What strategies for public clouds improvement are successful?
<--- Score

124. Do you combine technical expertise with business knowledge and public clouds Key topics include lifecycles, development approaches, requirements and how to make a business case?
<--- Score

125. What assumptions are made about the solution and approach?
<--- Score

126. How does your organization evaluate strategic public clouds success?
<--- Score

127. How do you go about comparing public clouds approaches/solutions?
<--- Score

128. What is public clouds risk?
<--- Score

129. How do you mitigate public clouds risk?
<--- Score

130. What is the magnitude of the improvements?
<--- Score

131. How is knowledge sharing about risk management improved?
<--- Score

132. Would you develop a public clouds Communication Strategy?
<--- Score

133. What are the affordable public clouds risks?
<--- Score

134. Risk Identification: What are the possible risk events your organization faces in relation to public clouds?
<--- Score

135. Risk events: what are the things that could go wrong?
<--- Score

Add up total points for this section:
_ _ _ _ _ = Total points for this section

Divided by: _ _ _ _ _ _ (number of statements answered) = _ _ _ _ _ _
Average score for this section

Transfer your score to the public clouds Index at the beginning of the Self-Assessment.

CRITERION #6: CONTROL:

INTENT: Implement the practical solution. Maintain the performance and correct possible complications.

In my belief, the answer to this question is clearly defined:

5 Strongly Agree

4 Agree

3 Neutral

2 Disagree

1 Strongly Disagree

1. What are you attempting to measure/monitor?
<--- Score

2. Are documented procedures clear and easy to follow for the operators?
<--- Score

3. What are customers monitoring?
<--- Score

4. How likely is the current public clouds plan to come in on schedule or on budget?
<--- Score

5. Are the planned controls in place?
<--- Score

6. What other areas of the group might benefit from the public clouds team's improvements, knowledge, and learning?
<--- Score

7. Does the public clouds performance meet the customer's requirements?
<--- Score

8. How can you best use all of your knowledge repositories to enhance learning and sharing?
<--- Score

9. Who will be in control?
<--- Score

10. What other systems, operations, processes, and infrastructures (hiring practices, staffing, training, incentives/rewards, metrics/dashboards/scorecards, etc.) need updates, additions, changes, or deletions in order to facilitate knowledge transfer and improvements?
<--- Score

11. Has the public clouds value of standards been quantified?
<--- Score

12. Against what alternative is success being measured?
<--- Score

13. Do you monitor the public clouds decisions made and fine tune them as they evolve?
<--- Score

14. Is there an action plan in case of emergencies?
<--- Score

15. Does job training on the documented procedures need to be part of the process team's education and training?
<--- Score

16. Are new process steps, standards, and documentation ingrained into normal operations?
<--- Score

17. How might the group capture best practices and lessons learned so as to leverage improvements?
<--- Score

18. Are pertinent alerts monitored, analyzed and distributed to appropriate personnel?
<--- Score

19. Who has control over resources?
<--- Score

20. How is public clouds project cost planned, managed, monitored?
<--- Score

21. Is new knowledge gained imbedded in the

response plan?

<--- Score

22. Is there documentation that will support the successful operation of the improvement?

<--- Score

23. Is a response plan in place for when the input, process, or output measures indicate an 'out-of-control' condition?

<--- Score

24. Who controls critical resources?

<--- Score

25. What are the key elements of your public clouds performance improvement system, including your evaluation, organizational learning, and innovation processes?

<--- Score

26. Is the public clouds test/monitoring cost justified?

<--- Score

27. What is the best design framework for public clouds organization now that, in a post industrial-age if the top-down, command and control model is no longer relevant?

<--- Score

28. How do you plan on providing proper recognition and disclosure of supporting companies?

<--- Score

29. What are the performance and scale of the public clouds tools?

<--- Score

30. How will new or emerging customer needs/
requirements be checked/communicated to orient
the process toward meeting the new specifications
and continually reducing variation?
<--- Score

31. What is the control/monitoring plan?
<--- Score

32. What can you control?
<--- Score

33. Is knowledge gained on process shared and
institutionalized?
<--- Score

34. In the case of a public clouds project, the criteria
for the audit derive from implementation objectives,
an audit of a public clouds project involves assessing
whether the recommendations outlined for
implementation have been met, can you track that
any public clouds project is implemented as planned,
and is it working?
<--- Score

35. Who is going to spread your message?
<--- Score

36. How will the day-to-day responsibilities for
monitoring and continual improvement be
transferred from the improvement team to the
process owner?
<--- Score

37. Are the planned controls working?
<--- Score

38. What is your theory of human motivation, and how does your compensation plan fit with that view?
<--- Score

39. Are the public clouds standards challenging?
<--- Score

40. Do the viable solutions scale to future needs?
<--- Score

41. Is there a public clouds Communication plan covering who needs to get what information when?
<--- Score

42. Is there a recommended audit plan for routine surveillance inspections of public clouds's gains?
<--- Score

43. Will existing staff require re-training, for example, to learn new business processes?
<--- Score

44. Do you establish a private (or community) cloud as a staging platform as you learn more about public clouds?
<--- Score

45. Is there a transfer of ownership and knowledge to process owner and process team tasked with the responsibilities.
<--- Score

46. Are you measuring, monitoring and predicting

public clouds activities to optimize operations and profitability, and enhancing outcomes?
<--- Score

47. You may have created your quality measures at a time when you lacked resources, technology wasn't up to the required standard, or low service levels were the industry norm. Have those circumstances changed?
<--- Score

48. What key inputs and outputs are being measured on an ongoing basis?
<--- Score

49. Has the improved process and its steps been standardized?
<--- Score

50. How do your controls stack up?
<--- Score

51. Implementation Planning: is a pilot needed to test the changes before a full roll out occurs?
<--- Score

52. Do you monitor the effectiveness of your public clouds activities?
<--- Score

53. Are controls in place and consistently applied?
<--- Score

54. How will report readings be checked to effectively monitor performance?
<--- Score

55. What are the critical parameters to watch?
<--- Score

56. Will the team be available to assist members in planning investigations?
<--- Score

57. How will the process owner verify improvement in present and future sigma levels, process capabilities?
<--- Score

58. How do senior leaders actions reflect a commitment to the organizations public clouds values?
<--- Score

59. How will the process owner and team be able to hold the gains?
<--- Score

60. What adjustments to the strategies are needed?
<--- Score

61. How is change control managed?
<--- Score

62. What do you stand for--and what are you against?
<--- Score

63. Where do ideas that reach policy makers and planners as proposals for public clouds strengthening and reform actually originate?
<--- Score

64. How do you monitor usage and cost?

<--- Score

65. Are suggested corrective/restorative actions indicated on the response plan for known causes to problems that might surface?
<--- Score

66. How widespread is its use?
<--- Score

67. Does a troubleshooting guide exist or is it needed?
<--- Score

68. Are there documented procedures?
<--- Score

69. Who is the public clouds process owner?
<--- Score

70. Is there a standardized process?
<--- Score

71. Do the public clouds decisions you make today help people and the planet tomorrow?
<--- Score

72. Are operating procedures consistent?
<--- Score

73. How do you plan for the cost of succession?
<--- Score

74. Does the response plan contain a definite closed loop continual improvement scheme (e.g., plan-do-check-act)?
<--- Score

75. What should you measure to verify efficiency gains?
<--- Score

76. What do your reports reflect?
<--- Score

77. How will input, process, and output variables be checked to detect for sub-optimal conditions?
<--- Score

78. How will you measure your QA plan's effectiveness?
<--- Score

79. What are the known security controls?
<--- Score

80. What is the recommended frequency of auditing?
<--- Score

81. How do you establish and deploy modified action plans if circumstances require a shift in plans and rapid execution of new plans?
<--- Score

82. Act/Adjust: What Do you Need to Do Differently?
<--- Score

83. Can support from partners be adjusted?
<--- Score

84. Is reporting being used or needed?
<--- Score

85. What quality tools were useful in the control phase?
<--- Score

86. What is your plan to assess your security risks?
<--- Score

87. Can you adapt and adjust to changing public clouds situations?
<--- Score

88. Will any special training be provided for results interpretation?
<--- Score

89. What do you measure to verify effectiveness gains?
<--- Score

90. What should the next improvement project be that is related to public clouds?
<--- Score

91. Have new or revised work instructions resulted?
<--- Score

92. Is there a control plan in place for sustaining improvements (short and long-term)?
<--- Score

93. How do you encourage people to take control and responsibility?
<--- Score

94. What are your results for key measures or indicators of the accomplishment of your public

clouds strategy and action plans, including building and strengthening core competencies?
<--- Score

95. How do you select, collect, align, and integrate public clouds data and information for tracking daily operations and overall organizational performance, including progress relative to strategic objectives and action plans?
<--- Score

96. Is there a documented and implemented monitoring plan?
<--- Score

97. How do you spread information?
<--- Score

98. Is a response plan established and deployed?
<--- Score

99. How do controls support value?
<--- Score

Add up total points for this section:
_ _ _ _ _ = Total points for this section

Divided by: _ _ _ _ _ _ (number of
statements answered) = _ _ _ _ _ _
Average score for this section

Transfer your score to the public clouds Index at the beginning of the Self-Assessment.

CRITERION #7: SUSTAIN:

INTENT: Retain the benefits.

In my belief, the answer to this
question is clearly defined:

5 Strongly Agree

4 Agree

3 Neutral

2 Disagree

1 Strongly Disagree

1. What threat is public clouds addressing?
<--- Score

2. How do you make it meaningful in connecting
public clouds with what users do day-to-day?
<--- Score

3. Are you satisfied with your current role? If not, what
is missing from it?
<--- Score

4. Is public clouds realistic, or are you setting yourself up for failure?
<--- Score

5. How important is public clouds to the user organizations mission?
<--- Score

6. What are the gaps in your knowledge and experience?
<--- Score

7. How do you maintain public clouds's Integrity?
<--- Score

8. Did your employees make progress today?
<--- Score

9. Why not do public clouds?
<--- Score

10. How can you incorporate support to ensure safe and effective use of public clouds into the services that you provide?
<--- Score

11. How will you insure seamless interoperability of public clouds moving forward?
<--- Score

12. How can you negotiate public clouds successfully with a stubborn boss, an irate client, or a deceitful coworker?
<--- Score

13. How will you know that the public clouds project

has been successful?
<--- Score

14. If you had to leave your organization for a year and the only communication you could have with employees/colleagues was a single paragraph, what would you write?
<--- Score

15. Will there be any necessary staff changes (redundancies or new hires)?
<--- Score

16. How do you assess the public clouds pitfalls that are inherent in implementing it?
<--- Score

17. How do you keep the momentum going?
<--- Score

18. What potential megatrends could make your business model obsolete?
<--- Score

19. What management system can you use to leverage the public clouds experience, ideas, and concerns of the people closest to the work to be done?
<--- Score

20. What are internal and external public clouds relations?
<--- Score

21. What you are going to do to affect the numbers?
<--- Score

22. How do you lead with public clouds in mind?
<--- Score

23. What unique value proposition (UVP) do you offer?
<--- Score

24. Do you think public clouds accomplishes the goals you expect it to accomplish?
<--- Score

25. How do you cross-sell and up-sell your public clouds success?
<--- Score

26. What happens if you do not have enough funding?
<--- Score

27. Is your strategy driving your strategy? Or is the way in which you allocate resources driving your strategy?
<--- Score

28. Is there any existing public clouds governance structure?
<--- Score

29. Whom among your colleagues do you trust, and for what?
<--- Score

30. What could happen if you do not do it?
<--- Score

31. If you got fired and a new hire took your place,

what would she do different?
<--- Score

32. What are you challenging?
<--- Score

33. Will it be accepted by users?
<--- Score

34. What are the success criteria that will indicate
that public clouds objectives have been met and the
benefits delivered?
<--- Score

35. Are there any activities that you can take off your
to do list?
<--- Score

36. What is the kind of project structure that would
be appropriate for your public clouds project, should
it be formal and complex, or can it be less formal and
relatively simple?
<--- Score

37. How do senior leaders deploy your organizations
vision and values through your leadership system, to
the workforce, to key suppliers and partners, and to
customers and other stakeholders, as appropriate?
<--- Score

38. Which individuals, teams or departments will be
involved in public clouds?
<--- Score

39. What are strategies for increasing support and
reducing opposition?

<--- Score

40. Is public clouds dependent on the successful delivery of a current project?
<--- Score

41. What stupid rule would you most like to kill?
<--- Score

42. What is it like to work for you?
<--- Score

43. What are the essentials of internal public clouds management?
<--- Score

44. Can the schedule be done in the given time?
<--- Score

45. Is the public clouds organization completing tasks effectively and efficiently?
<--- Score

46. What is the craziest thing you can do?
<--- Score

47. Think of your public clouds project, what are the main functions?
<--- Score

48. Marketing budgets are tighter, consumers are more skeptical, and social media has changed forever the way we talk about public clouds, how do you gain traction?
<--- Score

49. Who will be responsible for deciding whether public clouds goes ahead or not after the initial investigations?
<--- Score

50. What are the top 3 things at the forefront of your public clouds agendas for the next 3 years?
<--- Score

51. How do you go about securing public clouds?
<--- Score

52. How do you listen to customers to obtain actionable information?
<--- Score

53. Who are your customers?
<--- Score

54. What is the purpose of public clouds in relation to the mission?
<--- Score

55. How do you transition from the baseline to the target?
<--- Score

56. If your customer were your grandmother, would you tell her to buy what you're selling?
<--- Score

57. What projects are going on in the organization today, and what resources are those projects using from the resource pools?
<--- Score

58. Have new benefits been realized?
<--- Score

59. What is the overall talent health of your organization as a whole at senior levels, and for each organization reporting to a member of the Senior Leadership Team?
<--- Score

60. What does your signature ensure?
<--- Score

61. In retrospect, of the projects that you pulled the plug on, what percent do you wish had been allowed to keep going, and what percent do you wish had ended earlier?
<--- Score

62. What is your BATNA (best alternative to a negotiated agreement)?
<--- Score

63. What would have to be true for the option on the table to be the best possible choice?
<--- Score

64. What happens when a new employee joins the organization?
<--- Score

65. How is implementation research currently incorporated into each of your goals?
<--- Score

66. How do you deal with public clouds changes?
<--- Score

67. In the past year, what have you done (or could you have done) to increase the accurate perception of your company/brand as ethical and honest?
<--- Score

68. If you do not follow, then how to lead?
<--- Score

69. Are the assumptions believable and achievable?
<--- Score

70. How do you engage the workforce, in addition to satisfying them?
<--- Score

71. Who is responsible for public clouds?
<--- Score

72. Can you maintain your growth without detracting from the factors that have contributed to your success?
<--- Score

73. Which public clouds and CSPs is your business using?
<--- Score

74. Ask yourself: how would you do this work if you only had one staff member to do it?
<--- Score

75. Who have you, as a company, historically been when you've been at your best?
<--- Score

76. Are you using a design thinking approach and integrating Innovation, public clouds Experience, and Brand Value?
<--- Score

77. Which models, tools and techniques are necessary?
<--- Score

78. What are the business goals public clouds is aiming to achieve?
<--- Score

79. How do you provide a safe environment -physically and emotionally?
<--- Score

80. How do you track customer value, profitability or financial return, organizational success, and sustainability?
<--- Score

81. Is the impact that public clouds has shown?
<--- Score

82. How much contingency will be available in the budget?
<--- Score

83. Who is responsible for ensuring appropriate resources (time, people and money) are allocated to public clouds?
<--- Score

84. Are your responses positive or negative?
<--- Score

85. Do you have enough freaky customers in your portfolio pushing you to the limit day in and day out?
<--- Score

86. What was the last experiment you ran?
<--- Score

87. Do you think you know, or do you know you know ?
<--- Score

88. What role does communication play in the success or failure of a public clouds project?
<--- Score

89. What are you trying to prove to yourself, and how might it be hijacking your life and business success?
<--- Score

90. What is the source of the strategies for public clouds strengthening and reform?
<--- Score

91. If you had to rebuild your organization without any traditional competitive advantages (i.e., no killer technology, promising research, innovative product/ service delivery model, etcetera), how would your people have to approach their work and collaborate together in order to create the necessary conditions for success?
<--- Score

92. What information is critical to your organization that your executives are ignoring?
<--- Score

93. In a project to restructure public clouds outcomes, which stakeholders would you involve?
<--- Score

94. What are your most important goals for the strategic public clouds objectives?
<--- Score

95. Who will manage the integration of tools?
<--- Score

96. How do you stay inspired?
<--- Score

97. Can you do all this work?
<--- Score

98. Are you / should you be revolutionary or evolutionary?
<--- Score

99. If you were responsible for initiating and implementing major changes in your organization, what steps might you take to ensure acceptance of those changes?
<--- Score

100. What have been your experiences in defining long range public clouds goals?
<--- Score

101. What is the funding source for this project?
<--- Score

102. Is there a work around that you can use?

<--- Score

103. What trouble can you get into?
<--- Score

104. Why will customers want to buy your organizations products/services?
<--- Score

105. Do you have the right capabilities and capacities?
<--- Score

106. What are the usability implications of public clouds actions?
<--- Score

107. Who, on the executive team or the board, has spoken to a customer recently?
<--- Score

108. If your company went out of business tomorrow, would anyone who doesn't get a paycheck here care?
<--- Score

109. Do you have the right people on the bus?
<--- Score

110. How do customers see your organization?
<--- Score

111. Who do we want your customers to become?
<--- Score

112. Do public clouds rules make a reasonable demand on a users capabilities?
<--- Score

113. What is a feasible sequencing of reform initiatives over time?
<--- Score

114. How do you ensure that implementations of public clouds products are done in a way that ensures safety?
<--- Score

115. What is an unauthorized commitment?
<--- Score

116. When information truly is ubiquitous, when reach and connectivity are completely global, when computing resources are infinite, and when a whole new set of impossibilities are not only possible, but happening, what will that do to your business?
<--- Score

117. What are the potential basics of public clouds fraud?
<--- Score

118. How do you foster the skills, knowledge, talents, attributes, and characteristics you want to have?
<--- Score

119. How do you set public clouds stretch targets and how do you get people to not only participate in setting these stretch targets but also that they strive to achieve these?
<--- Score

120. How will you motivate the stakeholders with the least vested interest?

<--- Score

121. Where can you break convention?
<--- Score

122. What did you miss in the interview for the worst hire you ever made?
<--- Score

123. To whom do you add value?
<--- Score

124. Do you know what you are doing? And who do you call if you don't?
<--- Score

125. How do you govern and fulfill your societal responsibilities?
<--- Score

126. How are you doing compared to your industry?
<--- Score

127. Who do you want your customers to become?
<--- Score

128. Is it economical; do you have the time and money?
<--- Score

129. What is effective public clouds?
<--- Score

130. What is the overall business strategy?
<--- Score

131. What are the key enablers to make this public clouds move?
<--- Score

132. How do you manage public clouds Knowledge Management (KM)?
<--- Score

133. What are the barriers to increased public clouds production?
<--- Score

134. How long will it take to change?
<--- Score

135. What do we do when new problems arise?
<--- Score

136. How do you foster innovation?
<--- Score

137. What is your question? Why?
<--- Score

138. What trophy do you want on your mantle?
<--- Score

139. If you weren't already in this business, would you enter it today? And if not, what are you going to do about it?
<--- Score

140. What happens at your organization when people fail?
<--- Score

141. Are new benefits received and understood?
<--- Score

142. How can you become the company that would put you out of business?
<--- Score

143. What one word do you want to own in the minds of your customers, employees, and partners?
<--- Score

144. Why do and why don't your customers like your organization?
<--- Score

145. What is your formula for success in public clouds ?
<--- Score

146. Do you have an implicit bias for capital investments over people investments?
<--- Score

147. Operational - will it work?
<--- Score

148. What will be the consequences to the stakeholder (financial, reputation etc) if public clouds does not go ahead or fails to deliver the objectives?
<--- Score

149. How do you keep records, of what?
<--- Score

150. What public clouds skills are most important?
<--- Score

151. What are the short and long-term public clouds goals?
<--- Score

152. Which functions and people interact with the supplier and or customer?
<--- Score

153. Who do you think the world wants your organization to be?
<--- Score

154. At what moment would you think; Will I get fired?
<--- Score

155. What are specific public clouds rules to follow?
<--- Score

156. Can you break it down?
<--- Score

157. Is your basic point _____ or _____?
<--- Score

158. Is there any reason to believe the opposite of my current belief?
<--- Score

159. Do you see more potential in people than they do in themselves?
<--- Score

160. What knowledge, skills and characteristics mark a good public clouds project manager?
<--- Score

161. If no one would ever find out about your accomplishments, how would you lead differently?
<--- Score

162. What are current public clouds paradigms?
<--- Score

163. Are you relevant? Will you be relevant five years from now? Ten?
<--- Score

164. Do you say no to customers for no reason?
<--- Score

165. Have benefits been optimized with all key stakeholders?
<--- Score

166. If you find that you havent accomplished one of the goals for one of the steps of the public clouds strategy, what will you do to fix it?
<--- Score

167. How do you accomplish your long range public clouds goals?
<--- Score

168. Are assumptions made in public clouds stated explicitly?
<--- Score

169. Why is it important to have senior management support for a public clouds project?
<--- Score

170. Are you paying enough attention to the partners your company depends on to succeed?
<--- Score

171. What must you excel at?
<--- Score

172. Is maximizing public clouds protection the same as minimizing public clouds loss?
<--- Score

173. What are your personal philosophies regarding public clouds and how do they influence your work?
<--- Score

174. On-premise and/or public clouds?
<--- Score

175. Are all key stakeholders present at all Structured Walkthroughs?
<--- Score

176. What counts that you are not counting?
<--- Score

177. How does public clouds integrate with other stakeholder initiatives?
<--- Score

178. Do you feel that more should be done in the public clouds area?
<--- Score

179. What is your competitive advantage?
<--- Score

180. Would you rather sell to knowledgeable and informed customers or to uninformed customers?
<--- Score

181. How do you proactively clarify deliverables and public clouds quality expectations?
<--- Score

182. What have you done to protect your business from competitive encroachment?
<--- Score

183. How likely is it that a customer would recommend your company to a friend or colleague?
<--- Score

184. Has implementation been effective in reaching specified objectives so far?
<--- Score

185. What is the estimated value of the project?
<--- Score

186. What new services of functionality will be implemented next with public clouds ?
<--- Score

187. Who is responsible for errors?
<--- Score

188. What is the big public clouds idea?
<--- Score

189. How do you determine the key elements that affect public clouds workforce satisfaction, how are these elements determined for different workforce

groups and segments?
<--- Score

190. What public clouds modifications can you make work for you?
<--- Score

191. How can you become more high-tech but still be high touch?
<--- Score

192. Is a public clouds team work effort in place?
<--- Score

193. Who uses your product in ways you never expected?
<--- Score

194. If there were zero limitations, what would you do differently?
<--- Score

195. Why should people listen to you?
<--- Score

196. What is your public clouds strategy?
<--- Score

197. Why should you adopt a public clouds framework?
<--- Score

198. What business benefits will public clouds goals deliver if achieved?
<--- Score

199. How do you create buy-in?
<--- Score

200. Who will determine interim and final deadlines?
<--- Score

201. How do you know if you are successful?
<--- Score

202. How will you ensure you get what you expected?
<--- Score

203. Who is on the team?
<--- Score

204. Were lessons learned captured and communicated?
<--- Score

205. Whose voice (department, ethnic group, women, older workers, etc) might you have missed hearing from in your company, and how might you amplify this voice to create positive momentum for your business?
<--- Score

206. Are you changing as fast as the world around you?
<--- Score

207. What should you stop doing?
<--- Score

208. What are the long-term public clouds goals?
<--- Score

209. What is the recommended frequency of auditing?
<--- Score

210. What is the range of capabilities?
<--- Score

211. Are the criteria for selecting recommendations stated?
<--- Score

212. Do you have past public clouds successes?
<--- Score

213. Are you making progress, and are you making progress as public clouds leaders?
<--- Score

214. Which public clouds goals are the most important?
<--- Score

215. Who are four people whose careers you have enhanced?
<--- Score

Add up total points for this section:
_ _ _ _ _ = Total points for this section

Divided by: _ _ _ _ _ _ (number of statements answered) = _ _ _ _ _ _
Average score for this section

Transfer your score to the public clouds Index at the beginning of the Self-Assessment.

Public Clouds and Managing Projects, Criteria for Project Managers:

1.0 Initiating Process Group: Public Clouds

1. Do you know the Public Clouds projects goal, purpose and objectives?

2. Are there resources to maintain and support the outcome of the Public Clouds project?

3. Were resources available as planned?

4. What is the NEXT thing to do?

5. Were decisions made in a timely manner?

6. Did the Public Clouds project team have the right skills?

7. What do they need to know about the Public Clouds project?

8. Who are the Public Clouds project stakeholders?

9. Measurable - are the targets measurable?

10. Which six sigma dmaic phase focuses on why and how defects and errors occur?

11. During which stage of Risk planning are risks prioritized based on probability and impact?

12. How do you help others satisfy needs?

13. Are identified risks being monitored properly, are new risks arising during the Public Clouds project or

are foreseen risks occurring?

14. What will you do to minimize the impact should a risk event occur?

15. What technical work to do in each phase?

16. What do you need to do?

17. Did you use a contractor or vendor?

18. Information sharing?

19. How will you know you did it?

20. Who is funding the Public Clouds project?

1.1 Project Charter: Public Clouds

21. Environmental stewardship and sustainability considerations: what is the process that will be used to ensure compliance with the environmental stewardship policy?

22. Name and describe the elements that deal with providing the detail?

23. Review the general mission What system will be affected by the improvement efforts?

24. How do you manage integration?

25. Assumptions: what factors, for planning purposes, are you considering to be true?

26. What is the justification?

27. Why executive support?

28. Customer benefits: what customer requirements does this Public Clouds project address?

29. What are the assigned resources?

30. Who manages integration?

31. Success determination factors: how will the success of the Public Clouds project be determined from the customers perspective?

32. Assumptions and constraints: what assumptions

were made in defining the Public Clouds project?

33. What material?

34. Is time of the essence?

35. Pop quiz – which are the same inputs as in the Public Clouds project charter?

36. Run it as as a startup?

37. Are you building in-house ?

38. Major high-level milestone targets: what events measure progress?

39. Why the improvements?

1.2 Stakeholder Register: Public Clouds

40. Who wants to talk about Security?

41. Who is managing stakeholder engagement?

42. How will reports be created?

43. How should employers make voices heard?

44. What opportunities exist to provide communications?

45. What are the major Public Clouds project milestones requiring communications or providing communications opportunities?

46. How much influence do they have on the Public Clouds project?

47. Is your organization ready for change?

48. What & Why?

49. How big is the gap?

50. Who are the stakeholders?

51. What is the power of the stakeholder?

1.3 Stakeholder Analysis Matrix: Public Clouds

52. Political effects?

53. What is your Risk Management?

54. Global influences?

55. Location and geographical?

56. Are you going to weigh the stakeholders?

57. Loss of key staff?

58. Vulnerable groups; who are the vulnerable groups that might be affected by the Public Clouds project?

59. What is your Advocacy Strategy?

60. Would it be fair to say that cost is a controlling criteria?

61. New technologies, services, ideas?

62. Do the stakeholders goals and expectations support or conflict with the Public Clouds project goals?

63. Who determines value?

64. Partnership opportunities/synergies?

65. How do rules, behaviors affect stakes?

66. What tools would help you communicate?

67. What is the issue at stake?

68. What can the stakeholder prevent from happening?

69. Financial reserves, likely returns?

70. What mechanisms are proposed to monitor and measure Public Clouds project performance in terms of social development outcomes?

71. Market demand?

2.0 Planning Process Group: Public Clouds

72. Is your organization showing technical capacity and leadership commitment to keep working with the Public Clouds project and to repeat it?

73. Will the products created live up to the necessary quality?

74. In what ways can the governance of the Public Clouds project be improved so that it has greater likelihood of achieving future sustainability?

75. Do the partners have sufficient financial capacity to keep up the benefits produced by the programme?

76. Have operating capacities been created and/or reinforced in partners?

77. Are the necessary foundations in place to ensure the sustainability of the results of the Public Clouds project?

78. To what extent and in what ways are the Public Clouds project contributing to progress towards organizational reform?

79. How will you do it?

80. How should needs be met?

81. Is the Public Clouds project making progress in

helping to achieve the set results?

82. Contingency planning. if a risk event occurs, what will you do?

83. If action is called for, what form should it take?

84. Does the program have follow-up mechanisms (to verify the quality of the products, punctuality of delivery, etc.) to measure progress in the achievement of the envisaged results?

85. How are it Public Clouds projects different?

86. Is the duration of the program sufficient to ensure a cycle that will Public Clouds project the sustainability of the interventions?

87. Why is it important to determine activity sequencing on Public Clouds projects?

88. Is the pace of implementing the products of the program ensuring the completeness of the results of the Public Clouds project?

89. Are there efficient coordination mechanisms to avoid overloading the counterparts, participating stakeholders?

90. What do they need to know about the Public Clouds project?

91. Is the schedule for the set products being met?

2.1 Project Management Plan: Public Clouds

92. How do you manage time?

93. What does management expect of PMs?

94. Where does all this information come from?

95. Do the proposed changes from the Public Clouds project include any significant risks to safety?

96. Is there an incremental analysis/cost effectiveness analysis of proposed mitigation features based on an approved method and using an accepted model?

97. Will you add a schedule and diagram?

98. If the Public Clouds project is complex or scope is specialized, do you have appropriate and/or qualified staff available to perform the tasks?

99. Are the existing and future without-plan conditions reasonable and appropriate?

100. What would you do differently?

101. What went right?

102. What would you do differently what did not work?

103. What should you drop in order to add something

new?

104. Do there need to be organizational changes?

105. What are the known stakeholder requirements?

106. Are there non-structural buyout or relocation recommendations?

107. What data/reports/tools/etc. do program managers need?

108. What are the constraints?

109. Are there any client staffing expectations?

110. What are the assumptions?

111. Are comparable cost estimates used for comparing, screening and selecting alternative plans, and has a reasonable cost estimate been developed for the recommended plan?

2.2 Scope Management Plan: Public Clouds

112. Is it standard practice to formally commit stakeholders to the Public Clouds project via agreements?

113. Are the proposed Public Clouds project purposes different than the previously authorized Public Clouds project?

114. Function of the configuration control board?

115. What is your organizations history in doing similar activities?

116. Do you document disagreements and work towards resolutions?

117. Is documentation created for communication with the suppliers and Vendors?

118. Are mitigation strategies identified?

119. Time estimation – how much time will be needed?

120. Are schedule deliverables actually delivered?

121. Is the steering committee active in Public Clouds project oversight?

122. Is it possible to track all classes of Public Clouds

project work (e.g. scheduled, un-scheduled, defect repair, etc.)?

123. How difficult will it be to do specific activities on this Public Clouds project?

124. Are internal Public Clouds project status meetings held at reasonable intervals?

125. What problem is being solved by delivering this Public Clouds project?

126. Are risk oriented checklists used during risk identification?

127. Have the procedures for identifying budget variances been followed?

128. How relevant is this attribute to this Public Clouds project or audit?

129. What work performance data will be captured?

130. What strengths do you have?

131. Are the Public Clouds project plans updated on a frequent basis?

2.3 Requirements Management Plan: Public Clouds

132. Is the user satisfied?

133. What performance metrics will be used?

134. What went wrong?

135. Who will finally present the work or product(s) for acceptance?

136. Do you really need to write this document at all?

137. Have stakeholders been instructed in the Change Control process?

138. Will the contractors involved take full responsibility?

139. Will you document changes to requirements?

140. Who will initially review the Public Clouds project work or products to ensure it meets the applicable acceptance criteria?

141. Did you use declarative statements?

142. Has the requirements team been instructed in the Change Control process?

143. How will bidders price evaluations be done, by deliverables, phases, or in a big bang?

144. The wbs is developed as part of a joint planning session. and how do you know that youhave done this right?

145. How knowledgeable is the team in the proposed application area?

146. What information regarding the Public Clouds project requirements will be reported?

147. Do you have an appropriate arrangement for meetings?

148. Is there formal agreement on who has authority to request a change in requirements?

149. Who came up with this requirement?

150. Do you know which stakeholders will participate in the requirements effort?

151. Does the Public Clouds project have a Change Control process?

2.4 Requirements Documentation: Public Clouds

152. How will requirements be documented and who signs off on them?

153. What are the potential disadvantages/ advantages?

154. What is the risk associated with the technology?

155. How much testing do you need to do to prove that your system is safe?

156. How much does requirements engineering cost?

157. What can tools do for us?

158. What is a show stopper in the requirements?

159. Does your organization restrict technical alternatives?

160. How does the proposed Public Clouds project contribute to the overall objectives of your organization?

161. If applicable; are there issues linked with the fact that this is an offshore Public Clouds project?

162. Where are business rules being captured?

163. Can the requirement be changed without a large

impact on other requirements?

164. What is effective documentation?

165. How will the proposed Public Clouds project help?

166. How will they be documented / shared?

167. What happens when requirements are wrong?

168. Can the requirements be checked?

169. Completeness. are all functions required by the customer included?

170. Is the requirement realistically testable?

171. Are there any requirements conflicts?

2.5 Requirements Traceability Matrix: Public Clouds

172. Why use a WBS?

173. How do you manage scope?

174. Will you use a Requirements Traceability Matrix?

175. How will it affect the stakeholders personally in career?

176. What percentage of Public Clouds projects are producing traceability matrices between requirements and other work products?

177. Describe the process for approving requirements so they can be added to the traceability matrix and Public Clouds project work can be performed. Will the Public Clouds project requirements become approved in writing?

178. Why do you manage scope?

179. Is there a requirements traceability process in place?

180. Do you have a clear understanding of all subcontracts in place?

181. How small is small enough?

182. What is the WBS?

183. What are the chronologies, contingencies, consequences, criteria?

2.6 Project Scope Statement: Public Clouds

184. Elements that deal with providing the detail?

185. Will the qa related information be reported regularly as part of the status reporting mechanisms?

186. Has a method and process for requirement tracking been developed?

187. Risks?

188. Are there adequate Public Clouds project control systems?

189. Has the format for tracking and monitoring schedules and costs been defined?

190. Are there issues that could affect the existing requirements for the result, service, or product if the scope changes?

191. Were potential customers involved early in the planning process?

192. Did your Public Clouds project ask for this?

193. How often will scope changes be reviewed?

194. Has everyone approved the Public Clouds projects scope statement?

195. How will you verify the accuracy of the work of the Public Clouds project, and what constitutes acceptance of the deliverables?

196. Is an issue management process documented and filed?

197. Is the plan for your organization of the Public Clouds project resources adequate?

198. Elements of scope management that deal with concept development ?

199. Do you anticipate new stakeholders joining the Public Clouds project over time?

200. Will the risk status be reported to management on a regular and frequent basis?

201. Is the Public Clouds project manager qualified and experienced in Public Clouds project management?

2.7 Assumption and Constraint Log: Public Clouds

202. Are there processes defining how software will be developed including development methods, overall timeline for development, software product standards, and traceability?

203. How many Public Clouds project staff does this specific process affect?

204. Have all involved stakeholders and work groups committed to the Public Clouds project?

205. How do you design an auditing system?

206. What weaknesses do you have?

207. Does the plan conform to standards?

208. Have adequate resources been provided by management to ensure Public Clouds project success?

209. No superfluous information or marketing narrative?

210. What worked well?

211. Violation trace: why ?

212. Has a Public Clouds project Communications Plan been developed?

213. Do documented requirements exist for all critical components and areas, including technical, business, interfaces, performance, security and conversion requirements?

214. Have you eliminated all duplicative tasks or manual efforts, where appropriate?

215. Is this process still needed?

216. Are funding and staffing resource estimates sufficiently detailed and documented for use in planning and tracking the Public Clouds project?

217. What if failure during recovery?

218. Are there ways to reduce the time it takes to get something approved?

219. Are there processes in place to ensure internal consistency between the source code components?

220. After observing execution of process, is it in compliance with the documented Plan?

221. Does the Public Clouds project have a formal Public Clouds project Plan?

2.8 Work Breakdown Structure: Public Clouds

222. How many levels?

223. When do you stop?

224. Can you make it?

225. Is it a change in scope?

226. How far down?

227. What is the probability of completing the Public Clouds project in less that xx days?

228. When does it have to be done?

229. How big is a work-package?

230. How much detail?

231. Why is it useful?

232. What is the probability that the Public Clouds project duration will exceed xx weeks?

233. Why would you develop a Work Breakdown Structure?

234. When would you develop a Work Breakdown Structure?

235. Who has to do it?

236. Where does it take place?

237. What has to be done?

238. How will you and your Public Clouds project team define the Public Clouds projects scope and work breakdown structure?

2.9 WBS Dictionary: Public Clouds

239. Budgeted cost for work performed?

240. Are Public Clouds projected overhead costs in each pool and the associated direct costs used as the basis for establishing interim rates for allocating overhead to contracts?

241. Budgets assigned to control accounts?

242. Changes in the current direct and Public Clouds projected base?

243. Is undistributed budget limited to contract effort which cannot yet be planned to CWBS elements at or below the level specified for reporting to the Government?

244. Does the contractor have procedures which permit identification of recurring or non-recurring costs as necessary?

245. Incurrence of actual indirect costs in excess of budgets, by element of expense?

246. Are data elements summarized through the functional organizational structure for progressively higher levels of management?

247. Authorization to proceed with all authorized work?

248. Are overhead costs budgets established on a

basis consistent with anticipated direct business base?

249. Should you have a test for each code module?

250. Are the bases and rates for allocating costs from each indirect pool to commercial work consistent with the already stated used to allocate corresponding costs to Government contracts?

251. Are current budgets resulting from changes to the authorized work and/or internal replanning, reconcilable to original budgets for specified reporting items?

252. Do the lines of authority for incurring indirect costs correspond to the lines of responsibility for management control of the same components of costs?

253. Is future work which cannot be planned in detail subdivided to the extent practicable for budgeting and scheduling purposes?

254. Do you need another level?

255. Does the contractors system provide for accurate cost accumulation and assignment to control accounts in a manner consistent with the budgets using recognized acceptable costing techniques?

256. Are retroactive changes to direct costs and indirect costs prohibited except for the correction of errors and routine accounting adjustments?

257. Does the accounting system provide a basis for

auditing records of direct costs chargeable to the contract?

2.10 Schedule Management Plan: Public Clouds

258. Are assumptions being identified, recorded, analyzed, qualified and closed?

259. Personnel with expertise?

260. Is there a Steering Committee in place?

261. Was the scope definition used in task sequencing?

262. Have all necessary approvals been obtained?

263. Has a resource management plan been created?

264. Cost / benefit analysis?

265. Public Clouds project definition & scope?

266. Does the resource management plan include a personnel development plan?

267. Goal: is the schedule feasible and at what cost?

268. Have all documents been archived in a Public Clouds project repository for each release?

269. Has the business need been clearly defined?

270. Are Public Clouds project leaders committed to this Public Clouds project full time?

271. Has a Public Clouds project Communications Plan been developed?

272. Does a documented Public Clouds project organizational policy & plan (i.e. governance model) exist?

273. Are software metrics formally captured, analyzed and used as a basis for other Public Clouds project estimates?

274. How are Public Clouds projects different from operations?

275. Is the critical path valid?

276. Have all involved Public Clouds project stakeholders and work groups committed to the Public Clouds project?

277. Are all payments made according to the contract(s)?

2.11 Activity List: Public Clouds

278. Is there anything planned that does not need to be here?

279. When do the individual activities need to start and finish?

280. How can the Public Clouds project be displayed graphically to better visualize the activities?

281. What did not go as well?

282. Where will it be performed?

283. Are the required resources available or need to be acquired?

284. Should you include sub-activities?

285. What is the probability the Public Clouds project can be completed in xx weeks?

286. Who will perform the work?

287. How will it be performed?

288. How do you determine the late start (LS) for each activity?

289. When will the work be performed?

290. What is the LF and LS for each activity?

291. What went well?

292. How difficult will it be to do specific activities on this Public Clouds project?

293. What are the critical bottleneck activities?

294. How should ongoing costs be monitored to try to keep the Public Clouds project within budget?

295. What are you counting on?

2.12 Activity Attributes: Public Clouds

296. How much activity detail is required?

297. Time for overtime?

298. How many resources do you need to complete the work scope within a limit of X number of days?

299. Activity: fair or not fair?

300. Does your organization of the data change its meaning?

301. Can more resources be added?

302. What activity do you think you should spend the most time on?

303. Resource is assigned to?

304. Which method produces the more accurate cost assignment?

305. Have you identified the Activity Leveling Priority code value on each activity?

306. What conclusions/generalizations can you draw from this?

307. What is missing?

308. Has management defined a definite timeframe for the turnaround or Public Clouds project window?

309. Are the required resources available?

310. Do you feel very comfortable with your prediction?

311. How difficult will it be to do specific activities on this Public Clouds project?

312. How else could the items be grouped?

2.13 Milestone List: Public Clouds

313. Legislative effects?

314. Competitive advantages?

315. Describe the concept of the technology, product or service that will be or has been developed. How will it be used?

316. Obstacles faced?

317. How difficult will it be to do specific activities on this Public Clouds project?

318. What is the market for your technology, product or service?

319. Do you foresee any technical risks or developmental challenges?

320. Milestone pages should display the UserID of the person who added the milestone. Does a report or query exist that provides this audit information?

321. What specific improvements did you make to the Public Clouds project proposal since the previous time?

322. Information and research?

323. Calculate how long can activity be delayed?

324. Effects on core activities, distraction?

325. How soon can the activity finish?

326. It is to be a narrative text providing the crucial aspects of your Public Clouds project proposal answering what, who, how, when and where?

327. Gaps in capabilities?

2.14 Network Diagram: Public Clouds

328. Exercise: what is the probability that the Public Clouds project duration will exceed xx weeks?

329. What activity must be completed immediately before this activity can start?

330. What is the completion time?

331. Will crashing x weeks return more in benefits than it costs?

332. Planning: who, how long, what to do?

333. What activities must occur simultaneously with this activity?

334. What activities must follow this activity?

335. What job or jobs precede it?

336. Can you calculate the confidence level?

337. Which type of network diagram allows you to depict four types of dependencies?

338. Review the logical flow of the network diagram. Take a look at which activities you have first and then sequence the activities. Do they make sense?

339. Are the gantt chart and/or network diagram updated periodically and used to assess the overall Public Clouds project timetable?

340. How confident can you be in your milestone dates and the delivery date?

341. Where do schedules come from?

342. If a current contract exists, can you provide the vendor name, contract start, and contract expiration date?

343. What controls the start and finish of a job?

344. What to do and When?

345. What is the probability of completing the Public Clouds project in less that xx days?

346. What job or jobs could run concurrently?

2.15 Activity Resource Requirements: Public Clouds

347. Other support in specific areas?

348. What is the Work Plan Standard?

349. Do you use tools like decomposition and rolling-wave planning to produce the activity list and other outputs?

350. When does monitoring begin?

351. Organizational Applicability?

352. Are there unresolved issues that need to be addressed?

353. How many signatures do you require on a check and does this match what is in your policy and procedures?

354. Which logical relationship does the PDM use most often?

355. How do you handle petty cash?

356. Anything else?

357. What are constraints that you might find during the Human Resource Planning process?

358. Why do you do that?

2.16 Resource Breakdown Structure: Public Clouds

359. What is the number one predictor of a groups productivity?

360. How difficult will it be to do specific activities on this Public Clouds project?

361. The list could probably go on, but, the thing that you would most like to know is, How long & How much?

362. What are the requirements for resource data?

363. How should the information be delivered?

364. What defines a successful Public Clouds project?

365. Who delivers the information?

366. What is the difference between % Complete and % work?

367. How can this help you with team building?

368. Who is allowed to perform which functions?

369. What is Public Clouds project communication management?

370. Why time management?

371. What defines a successful Public Clouds project?

372. What can you do to improve productivity?

373. What is the purpose of assigning and documenting responsibility?

374. Why do you do it?

375. When do they need the information?

376. Who will be used as a Public Clouds project team member?

2.17 Activity Duration Estimates: Public Clouds

377. What are the nine areas of expertise?

378. What is done after activity duration estimation?

379. What is the difference between using brainstorming and the Delphi technique for risk identification?

380. Will additional funds be needed for hardware or software?

381. Are reward and recognition systems defined to promote or reinforce desired behavior?

382. Describe a Public Clouds project that suffered from scope creep. Could it have been avoided?

383. How difficult will it be to complete specific activities on this Public Clouds project?

384. How does a Public Clouds project life cycle differ from a product life cycle?

385. Would you rate yourself as being risk-averse, risk-neutral, or risk-seeking?

386. Are time, scope, cost, and quality monitored throughout the Public Clouds project?

387. Account for the four frames of organizations.

How can they help Public Clouds project managers understand your organizational context for Public Clouds projects?

388. Which suggestions do you find most useful?

389. Are risks monitored to determine if an event has occurred or if the mitigation was successful?

390. Why should Public Clouds project managers strive to make jobs look easy?

391. Do procedures exist describing how the Public Clouds project scope will be managed?

392. List five reasons why organizations outsource. Why is there a growing trend in outsourcing, especially in the government?

393. Are Public Clouds project activities decomposed into manageable components to ensure expected management control?

394. Does a procedure exist to ensure the Public Clouds project work is completed in the appropriate sequence and on time?

395. What are the key components of a Public Clouds project communications plan?

396. What steps did your organization take to earn this prestigious quality award?

2.18 Duration Estimating Worksheet: Public Clouds

397. Can the Public Clouds project be constructed as planned?

398. Small or large Public Clouds project?

399. What is your role?

400. Why estimate time and cost?

401. What is the total time required to complete the Public Clouds project if no delays occur?

402. For other activities, how much delay can be tolerated?

403. Define the work as completely as possible. What work will be included in the Public Clouds project?

404. What info is needed?

405. Does the Public Clouds project provide innovative ways for stakeholders to overcome obstacles or deliver better outcomes?

406. What utility impacts are there?

407. How should ongoing costs be monitored to try to keep the Public Clouds project within budget?

408. When does your organization expect to be able

to complete it?

409. Value pocket identification & quantification what are value pockets?

410. How can the Public Clouds project be displayed graphically to better visualize the activities?

411. What is cost and Public Clouds project cost management?

412. When, then?

2.19 Project Schedule: Public Clouds

413. Why do you think schedule issues often cause the most conflicts on Public Clouds projects?

414. What is Public Clouds project management?

415. What is risk management?

416. Schedule/cost recovery?

417. Why or why not?

418. Are key risk mitigation strategies added to the Public Clouds project schedule?

419. Activity charts and bar charts are graphical representations of a Public Clouds project schedule ...how do they differ?

420. Month Public Clouds project take?

421. Are quality inspections and review activities listed in the Public Clouds project schedule(s)?

422. Are there activities that came from a template or previous Public Clouds project that are not applicable on this phase of this Public Clouds project?

423. Is the structure for tracking the Public Clouds project schedule well defined and assigned to a specific individual?

424. How can slack be negative?

425. How closely did the initial Public Clouds project Schedule compare with the actual schedule?

426. Does the condition or event threaten the Public Clouds projects objectives in any ways?

427. Have all Public Clouds project delays been adequately accounted for, communicated to all stakeholders and adjustments made in overall Public Clouds project schedule?

428. Why is software Public Clouds project disaster so common?

429. Master Public Clouds project schedule?

430. Public Clouds project work estimates Who is managing the work estimate quality of work tasks in the Public Clouds project schedule?

2.20 Cost Management Plan: Public Clouds

431. Have all unresolved risks been documented?

432. What is your organizations history in doing similar tasks?

433. For cost control purposes?

434. Is the communication plan being followed?

435. Are the schedule estimates reasonable given the Public Clouds project?

436. Are post milestone Public Clouds project reviews (PMPR) conducted with your organization at least once a year?

437. Are status reports received per the Public Clouds project Plan?

438. Exclusions – is there scope to be performed or provided by others?

439. Are vendor invoices audited for accuracy before payment?

440. Was the Public Clouds project schedule reviewed by all stakeholders and formally accepted?

441. Is the structure for tracking the Public Clouds project schedule well defined and assigned to a

specific individual?

442. Is current scope of the Public Clouds project substantially different than that originally defined?

443. Are changes in deliverable commitments agreed to by all affected groups & individuals?

444. Has a Public Clouds project Communications Plan been developed?

445. Are milestone deliverables effectively tracked and compared to Public Clouds project plan?

446. Contracting method – what contracting method is to be used for the contracts?

447. Are corrective actions and variances reported?

448. What is the work breakdown structure for the Public Clouds project?

449. Owner, contractor, and subcontractors?

450. What does this mean to a cost or scheduler manager?

2.21 Activity Cost Estimates: Public Clouds

451. Were the tasks or work products prepared by the consultant useful?

452. Padding is bad and contingencies are good. what is the difference?

453. Was the consultant knowledgeable about the program?

454. Did the consultant work with local staff to develop local capacity?

455. Is costing method consistent with study goals?

456. What happens if you cannot produce the documentation for the single audit?

457. How do you fund change orders?

458. How Award?

459. The impact and what actions were taken?

460. How many activities should you have?

461. Does the estimator estimate by task or by person?

462. What is the activity recast of the budget?

463. What is the estimators estimating history?

464. Were you satisfied with the work?

465. Who determines the quality and expertise of contractors?

466. What is a Public Clouds project Management Plan?

467. Does the activity use a common approach or business function to deliver its results?

468. Who & what determines the need for contracted services?

469. Vac -variance at completion, how much over/ under budget do you expect to be?

2.22 Cost Estimating Worksheet: Public Clouds

470. Does the Public Clouds project provide innovative ways for stakeholders to overcome obstacles or deliver better outcomes?

471. Identify the timeframe necessary to monitor progress and collect data to determine how the selected measure has changed?

472. Will the Public Clouds project collaborate with the local community and leverage resources?

473. Is the Public Clouds project responsive to community need?

474. Can a trend be established from historical performance data on the selected measure and are the criteria for using trend analysis or forecasting methods met?

475. What additional Public Clouds project(s) could be initiated as a result of this Public Clouds project?

476. What is the estimated labor cost today based upon this information?

477. What is the purpose of estimating?

478. Is it feasible to establish a control group arrangement?

479. What will others want?

480. What costs are to be estimated?

481. What happens to any remaining funds not used?

482. Who is best positioned to know and assist in identifying corresponding factors?

483. What can be included?

484. How will the results be shared and to whom?

485. Ask: are others positioned to know, are others credible, and will others cooperate?

2.23 Cost Baseline: Public Clouds

486. At which frequency ?

487. Are you asking management for something as a result of this update?

488. Does the suggested change request seem to represent a necessary enhancement to the product?

489. What does a good WBS NOT look like?

490. Has operations management formally accepted responsibility for operating and maintaining the product(s) or service(s) delivered by the Public Clouds project?

491. Have all the product or service deliverables been accepted by the customer?

492. What do you want to measure ?

493. Who will use corresponding metrics ?

494. Is the cr within Public Clouds project scope?

495. Definition of done can be traced back to the definitions of what are you providing to the customer in terms of deliverables?

496. How concrete were original objectives?

497. Does the suggested change request represent a desired enhancement to the products functionality?

498. If you sold 10x widgets on a day, what would the affect on profits be?

499. Impact to environment?

500. Are you meeting with your team regularly?

501. What deliverables come first?

502. Should a more thorough impact analysis be conducted?

2.24 Quality Management Plan: Public Clouds

503. Contradictory information between different documents?

504. How do senior leaders create and communicate values and performance expectations?

505. What is the return on investment?

506. How are training records kept?

507. How do you prioritize?

508. How do you field-modify testing procedures?

509. Does the Public Clouds project have a formal Public Clouds project Plan?

510. Are requirements management tracking tools and procedures in place?

511. What is quality planning ?

512. What are your organizations current levels and trends for the already stated measures related to employee wellbeing, satisfaction, and development?

513. How is staff trained?

514. How will you know that a change is actually an improvement?

515. What data do you gather/use/compile?

516. With the five whys method, the team considers why the issue being explored occurred. do others then take that initial answer and ask why?

517. How does your organization manage work to promote cooperation, individual initiative, innovation, flexibility, communications, and knowledge/skill sharing across work units?

518. What would you gain if you spent time working to improve this process?

519. Are there procedures in place to effectively manage interdependencies with other Public Clouds projects / systems?

520. Would impacts defined serve as impediments?

521. Why quality management?

522. Are you meeting your customers expectations consistently?

2.25 Quality Metrics: Public Clouds

523. Was review conducted per standard protocols?

524. When will the Final Guidance will be issued?

525. Were number of defects identified?

526. Is there alignment within your organization on definitions?

527. What are your organizations expectations for its quality Public Clouds project?

528. How exactly do you define when differences exist?

529. If the defect rate during testing is substantially higher than that of the previous release (or a similar product), then ask: Did you plan for and actually improve testing effectiveness?

530. What is the CMS Benchmark?

531. What happens if you get an abnormal result?

532. Is quality culture a competitive advantage?

533. How do you measure?

534. Does risk analysis documentation meet standards?

535. Do you know how much profit a 10% decrease in

waste would generate?

536. Has it met internal or external standards?

537. Are documents on hand to provide explanations of privacy and confidentiality?

538. What documentation is required?

539. Where is quality now?

540. Where did complaints, returns and warranty claims come from?

541. Are quality metrics defined?

542. What is the benchmark?

2.26 Process Improvement Plan: Public Clouds

543. Are you making progress on your improvement plan?

544. The motive is determined by asking, Why do you want to achieve this goal?

545. Purpose of goal: the motive is determined by asking, why do you want to achieve this goal?

546. What personnel are the champions for the initiative?

547. Are you meeting the quality standards?

548. What personnel are the coaches for your initiative?

549. Have the frequency of collection and the points in the process where measurements will be made been determined?

550. What lessons have you learned so far?

551. Have storage and access mechanisms and procedures been determined?

552. Are you making progress on the improvement framework?

553. Where do you focus?

554. Does explicit definition of the measures exist?

555. What personnel are the sponsors for that initiative?

556. What personnel are the change agents for your initiative?

557. Who should prepare the process improvement action plan?

558. Where do you want to be?

559. Are you following the quality standards?

560. Are you making progress on the goals?

2.27 Responsibility Assignment Matrix: Public Clouds

561. How cost benefit analysis?

562. Are all elements of indirect expense identified to overhead cost budgets of Public Clouds projections?

563. Actual cost of work performed?

564. Are the requirements for all items of overhead established by rational, traceable processes?

565. Is accountability placed at the lowest-possible level within the Public Clouds project so that decisions can be made at that level?

566. The already stated responsible for overhead performance control of related costs?

567. Detailed schedules which support control account and work package start and completion dates/events?

568. Availability – will the group or the person be available within the necessary time interval?

569. The anticipated business volume?

570. How many hours by each staff member/rate?

571. Do others have the time to dedicate to your Public Clouds project?

572. Past experience – the person or the group worked at something similar in the past?

573. If a role has only Signing-off, or only Communicating responsibility and has no Performing, Accountable, or Monitoring responsibility, is it necessary?

574. What do you need to implement earned value management?

575. What happens when others get pulled for higher priority Public Clouds projects?

576. Undistributed budgets, if any?

577. Does the contractor use objective results, design reviews and tests to trace schedule performance?

578. Is all contract work included in the CWBS?

579. Does each activity-deliverable have exactly one Accountable responsibility, so that accountability is clear and decisions can be made quickly?

2.28 Roles and Responsibilities: Public Clouds

580. Concern: where are you limited or have no authority, where you can not influence?

581. What is working well?

582. Where are you most strong as a supervisor?

583. What expectations were NOT met?

584. What specific behaviors did you observe?

585. How is your work-life balance?

586. What should you do now to ensure that you are exceeding expectations and excelling in your current position?

587. Who is involved?

588. Are Public Clouds project team roles and responsibilities identified and documented?

589. Required skills, knowledge, experience?

590. What is working well within your organizations performance management system?

591. What are your major roles and responsibilities in the area of performance measurement and assessment?

592. Accountabilities: what are the roles and responsibilities of individual team members?

593. What expectations were met?

594. Once the responsibilities are defined for the Public Clouds project, have the deliverables, roles and responsibilities been clearly communicated to every participant?

595. Once the responsibilities are defined for the Public Clouds project, have the deliverables, roles and responsibilities been clearly communicated to every participant?

596. Was the expectation clearly communicated?

597. Do you take the time to clearly define roles and responsibilities on Public Clouds project tasks?

598. Is there a training program in place for stakeholders covering expectations, roles and responsibilities and any addition knowledge others need to be good stakeholders?

2.29 Human Resource Management Plan: Public Clouds

599. Public Clouds project Objectives?

600. Are tasks tracked by hours?

601. What are the Staffing Requirements?

602. How are you going to ensure that you have a well motivated workforce?

603. Is Public Clouds project status reviewed with the steering and executive teams at appropriate intervals?

604. Timeline and milestones?

605. Does the schedule include Public Clouds project management time and change request analysis time?

606. Are the key elements of a Public Clouds project Charter present?

607. Are meeting minutes captured and sent out after the meeting?

608. Have activity relationships and interdependencies within tasks been adequately identified?

609. Are change requests logged and managed?

610. How does the proposed individual meet each

requirement?

611. Has the Public Clouds project manager been identified?

612. Have the key elements of a coherent Public Clouds project management strategy been established?

613. Specific - is the objective clear in terms of what, how, when, and where the situation will be changed?

614. Is the structure for tracking the Public Clouds project schedule well defined and assigned to a specific individual?

615. What is this Public Clouds project aiming to achieve?

616. Are the right people being attracted and retained to meet the future challenges?

2.30 Communications Management Plan: Public Clouds

617. Who to share with?

618. What data is going to be required?

619. In your work, how much time is spent on stakeholder identification?

620. Where do team members get information?

621. How often do you engage with stakeholders?

622. How do you manage communications?

623. Are you constantly rushing from meeting to meeting?

624. Do you ask; can you recommend others for you to talk with about this initiative?

625. What help do you and your team need from the stakeholder?

626. Do you feel more overwhelmed by stakeholders?

627. What is the stakeholders level of authority?

628. Are there potential barriers between the team and the stakeholder?

629. Who to learn from?

630. Who were proponents/opponents?

631. Which stakeholders are thought leaders, influences, or early adopters?

632. How much time does it take to do it?

633. Who is involved as you identify stakeholders?

634. Who have you worked with in past, similar initiatives?

635. What communications method?

636. Who needs to know and how much?

2.31 Risk Management Plan: Public Clouds

637. Are the best people available?

638. Costs associated with late delivery or a defective product?

639. Workarounds are determined during which step of risk management?

640. What are some questions that should be addressed in a risk management plan?

641. Which risks should get the attention?

642. Are staff committed for the duration of the product?

643. Are testing tools available and suitable?

644. What are the cost, schedule and resource impacts if the risk does occur?

645. Is the customer willing to participate in reviews?

646. Are Public Clouds project requirements stable?

647. How can the process be made more effective or less cumbersome (process improvements)?

648. Risks should be identified during which phase of Public Clouds project management life cycle?

649. Does the Public Clouds project have the authority and ability to avoid the risk?

650. Was an original risk assessment/risk management plan completed?

651. Are you on schedule?

652. How much risk can you tolerate?

653. Are enough people available?

654. Is there anything you would now do differently on your Public Clouds project based on this experience?

655. For software; are compilers and code generators available and suitable for the product to be built?

2.32 Risk Register: Public Clouds

656. What can be done about it?

657. Are there any knock-on effects/impact on any of the other areas?

658. What would the impact to the Public Clouds project objectives be should the risk arise?

659. Risk categories: what are the main categories of risks that should be addressed on this Public Clouds project?

660. People risk -are people with appropriate skills available to help complete the Public Clouds project?

661. Contingency actions - planned actions to reduce the immediate seriousness of the risk when it does occur. What should you do when?

662. Which key risks have ineffective responses or outstanding improvement actions?

663. What are the assumptions and current status that support the assessment of the risk?

664. What is the probability and impact of the risk occurring?

665. Methodology: how will risk management be performed on this Public Clouds project?

666. Do you require further engagement?

667. What is the appropriate level of risk management for this Public Clouds project?

668. Financial risk -can your organization afford to undertake the Public Clouds project?

669. Can the likelihood and impact of failing to achieve corresponding recommendations and action plans be assessed?

670. Having taken action, how did the responses effect change, and where is the Public Clouds project now?

671. When would you develop a risk register?

672. What evidence do you have to justify the likelihood score of the risk (audit, incident report, claim, complaints, inspection, internal review)?

673. Budget and schedule: what are the estimated costs and schedules for performing risk-related activities?

674. Are there any gaps in the evidence?

675. Is further information required before making a decision?

2.33 Probability and Impact Assessment: Public Clouds

676. When and how will the recent breakthroughs in basic research lead to commercial products?

677. What action do you usually take against risks?

678. Are the software tools integrated with each other?

679. Is the delay in one subPublic Clouds project going to affect another?

680. Do you use diagramming techniques to show cause and effect?

681. Do benefits and chances of success outweigh potential damage if success is not attained?

682. Can you stabilize dynamic risk factors?

683. Have staff received necessary training?

684. What things are likely to change?

685. Is the process supported by tools?

686. Do you train all developers in the process?

687. Is the customer willing to establish rapid communication links with the developer?

688. Who has experience with this?

689. How will the consumption pattern change?

690. Can this technology be absorbed with current level of expertise available in your organization?

691. Anticipated volatility of the requirements?

692. What are the chances the risk event will occur?

693. Have top software and customer managers formally committed to support the Public Clouds project?

694. Has something like this been done before?

695. What are its business ethics?

2.34 Probability and Impact Matrix: Public Clouds

696. Does the customer have a solid idea of what is required?

697. Has the need for the Public Clouds project been properly established?

698. How will economic events and trends likely affect the Public Clouds project?

699. What do you expect?

700. Are there alternative opinions/solutions/processes you should explore?

701. Are there new risks that mitigation strategies might introduce?

702. What needs to be DONE?

703. Do the requirements require the creation of new algorithms?

704. Is there any sign of biased ranking?

705. Can the risk be avoided by choosing a different alternative?

706. Sensitivity analysis -which risks will have the most impact on the Public Clouds project?

707. How do you manage Public Clouds project Risk?

708. What will be the impact or consequence if the risk occurs?

709. Are team members trained in the use of the tools?

710. How completely has the customer been identified?

711. Do others match with the clients requirement?

712. Are Public Clouds project requirements stable?

713. Degree of confidence in estimated size estimate?

2.35 Risk Data Sheet: Public Clouds

714. How can hazards be reduced?

715. Risk of what?

716. What actions can be taken to eliminate or remove risk?

717. What was measured?

718. Do effective diagnostic tests exist?

719. What are you here for (Mission)?

720. During work activities could hazards exist?

721. What can you do?

722. What are you trying to achieve (Objectives)?

723. What can happen?

724. Who has a vested interest in how you perform as your organization (our stakeholders)?

725. Whom do you serve (customers)?

726. What are you weak at and therefore need to do better?

727. Potential for recurrence?

728. Has a sensitivity analysis been carried out?

729. What are the main threats to your existence?

730. What are your core values?

731. What is the likelihood of it happening?

732. Has the most cost-effective solution been chosen?

2.36 Procurement Management Plan: Public Clouds

733. Are the people assigned to the Public Clouds project sufficiently qualified?

734. Has the Public Clouds project manager been identified?

735. Is there a procurement management plan in place?

736. What is the last item a Public Clouds project manager must do to finalize Public Clouds project close-out?

737. Are Public Clouds project contact logs kept up to date?

738. Is a stakeholder management plan in place that covers topics?

739. How will you coordinate Procurement with aspects of the Public Clouds project?

740. Are adequate resources provided for the quality assurance function?

741. Has a sponsor been identified?

742. Are the appropriate IT resources adequate to meet planned commitments?

743. Is there a formal process for updating the Public Clouds project baseline?

744. Were Public Clouds project team members involved in the development of activity & task decomposition?

745. Are key risk mitigation strategies added to the Public Clouds project schedule?

746. Are risk triggers captured?

747. Do all stakeholders know how to access the PM repository and where to find the Public Clouds project documentation?

748. Is there a formal set of procedures supporting Stakeholder Management?

2.37 Source Selection Criteria: Public Clouds

749. What can not be disclosed?

750. When must you conduct a debriefing?

751. Can you prevent comparison of proposals?

752. What are the requirements for publicizing a RFP?

753. How and when do you enter into Public Clouds project Procurement Management?

754. How can business terms and conditions be improved to yield more effective price competition?

755. What information may not be provided?

756. What should preproposal conferences accomplish?

757. What aspects should the contracting officer brief the Public Clouds project on prior to evaluation of proposals?

758. What instructions should be provided regarding oral presentations?

759. What should a Draft Request for Proposal (DRFP) include?

760. When and what information can be considered

with offerors regarding past performance?

761. Will the technical evaluation factor unnecessarily force the acquisition into a higher-priced market segment?

762. What source selection software is your team using?

763. What should be considered?

764. What are the guiding principles for developing an evaluation report?

765. Who must be notified?

766. What are the most critical evaluation criteria that prove to be tiebreakers in the evaluation of proposals?

767. What past performance information should be requested?

768. Are considerations anticipated?

2.38 Stakeholder Management Plan: Public Clouds

769. Are software metrics formally captured, analyzed and used as a basis for other Public Clouds project estimates?

770. Has the Public Clouds project manager been identified?

771. How are you doing/what can be done better?

772. Are updated Public Clouds project time & resource estimates reasonable based on the current Public Clouds project stage?

773. Is the quality assurance team identified?

774. Are there cosmetic errors that hinder readability and comprehension?

775. Are Public Clouds project team members involved in detailed estimating and scheduling?

776. Have Public Clouds project success criteria been defined?

777. Is there a formal process for updating the Public Clouds project baseline?

778. What guidelines or procedures currently exist that must be adhered to (eg departmental accounting procedures)?

779. Is staff trained on the software technologies that are being used on the Public Clouds project?

780. What has to be purchased?

781. Are written status reports provided on a designated frequent basis?

782. Pareto diagrams, statistical sampling, flow charting or trend analysis used quality monitoring?

783. Alignment to strategic goals & objectives?

784. Does this include subcontracted development?

785. Are all resource assumptions documented?

2.39 Change Management Plan: Public Clouds

786. Has the training co-ordinator been provided with the training details and put in place the necessary arrangements?

787. How will you deal with anger about the restricting of communications due to confidentiality considerations?

788. What are the specific target groups/audiences that will be impacted by this change?

789. What are the training strategies?

790. Has the priority for this Public Clouds project been set by the Business Unit Management Team?

791. Who might present the most resistance?

792. What is the most positive interpretation it can receive?

793. What does a resilient organization look like?

794. Is there an adequate supply of people for the new roles?

795. What are you trying to achieve as a result of communication?

796. What method and medium would you use to

announce a message?

797. What work practices will be affected?

798. Where will the funds come from?

799. Is there support for this application(s) and are the details available for distribution?

800. How many people are required in each of the roles?

801. What do you expect the target audience to do, say, think or feel as a result of this communication?

802. What new roles are needed?

803. How much change management is needed?

804. When does it make sense to customize?

3.0 Executing Process Group: Public Clouds

805. Do the products created live up to the necessary quality?

806. How can software assist in Public Clouds project communications?

807. What are the Public Clouds project management deliverables of each process group?

808. How do you enter durations, link tasks, and view critical path information?

809. How can your organization use a weighted decision matrix to evaluate proposals as part of source selection?

810. What are the challenges Public Clouds project teams face?

811. What are deliverables of your Public Clouds project?

812. What areas does the group agree are the biggest success on the Public Clouds project?

813. Just how important is your work to the overall success of the Public Clouds project?

814. What is the shortest possible time it will take to complete this Public Clouds project?

815. How is Public Clouds project performance information created and distributed?

816. What are the typical Public Clouds project management skills?

817. If a risk event occurs, what will you do?

818. What good practices or successful experiences or transferable examples have been identified?

819. Were sponsors and decision makers available when needed outside regularly scheduled meetings?

820. How could you control progress of your Public Clouds project?

3.1 Team Member Status Report: Public Clouds

821. Are the attitudes of staff regarding Public Clouds project work improving?

822. How much risk is involved?

823. What is to be done?

824. What specific interest groups do you have in place?

825. How will resource planning be done?

826. When a teams productivity and success depend on collaboration and the efficient flow of information, what generally fails them?

827. How does this product, good, or service meet the needs of the Public Clouds project and your organization as a whole?

828. The problem with Reward & Recognition Programs is that the truly deserving people all too often get left out. How can you make it practical?

829. How can you make it practical?

830. Does every department have to have a Public Clouds project Manager on staff?

831. Do you have an Enterprise Public Clouds project

Management Office (EPMO)?

832. Why is it to be done?

833. Will the staff do training or is that done by a third party?

834. Is there evidence that staff is taking a more professional approach toward management of your organizations Public Clouds projects?

835. Does your organization have the means (staff, money, contract, etc.) to produce or to acquire the product, good, or service?

836. Are the products of your organizations Public Clouds projects meeting customers objectives?

837. How it is to be done?

838. Are your organizations Public Clouds projects more successful over time?

839. Does the product, good, or service already exist within your organization?

3.2 Change Request: Public Clouds

840. How to get changes (code) out in a timely manner?

841. How are changes graded and who is responsible for the rating?

842. What is the function of the change control committee?

843. What can be filed?

844. What is the purpose of change control?

845. How do team members communicate with each other?

846. How can you ensure that changes have been made properly?

847. Who needs to approve change requests?

848. Who is responsible to authorize changes?

849. How many lines of code must be changed to implement the change?

850. Are there requirements attributes that are strongly related to the occurrence of defects and failures?

851. How is the change documented (format, content, storage)?

852. What type of changes does change control take into account?

853. Who can suggest changes?

854. Why do you want to have a change control system?

855. Change request coordination ?

856. What are the basic mechanics of the Change Advisory Board (CAB)?

857. What are the duties of the change control team?

858. Can static requirements change attributes like the size of the change be used to predict reliability in execution?

3.3 Change Log: Public Clouds

859. Is the submitted change a new change or a modification of a previously approved change?

860. Where do changes come from?

861. When was the request submitted?

862. How does this change affect the timeline of the schedule?

863. Who initiated the change request?

864. Will the Public Clouds project fail if the change request is not executed?

865. Is the change request open, closed or pending?

866. Do the described changes impact on the integrity or security of the system?

867. When was the request approved?

868. Is the requested change request a result of changes in other Public Clouds project(s)?

869. Is the change backward compatible without limitations?

870. How does this relate to the standards developed for specific business processes?

871. Is this a mandatory replacement?

872. How does this change affect scope?

873. Is the change request within Public Clouds project scope?

3.4 Decision Log: Public Clouds

874. Which variables make a critical difference?

875. Does anything need to be adjusted?

876. How does the use a Decision Support System influence the strategies/tactics or costs?

877. How do you know when you are achieving it?

878. What eDiscovery problem or issue did your organization set out to fix or make better?

879. How does provision of information, both in terms of content and presentation, influence acceptance of alternative strategies?

880. What are the cost implications?

881. Meeting purpose; why does this team meet?

882. Decision-making process; how will the team make decisions?

883. What makes you different or better than others companies selling the same thing?

884. It becomes critical to track and periodically revisit both operational effectiveness; Are you noticing all that you need to, and are you interpreting what you see effectively?

885. How effective is maintaining the log at

facilitating organizational learning?

886. With whom was the decision shared or considered?

887. What is your overall strategy for quality control / quality assurance procedures?

888. Linked to original objective?

889. Do strategies and tactics aimed at less than full control reduce the costs of management or simply shift the cost burden?

890. How do you define success?

891. Who is the decisionmaker?

892. Behaviors; what are guidelines that the team has identified that will assist them with getting the most out of team meetings?

893. Is your opponent open to a non-traditional workflow, or will it likely challenge anything you do?

3.5 Quality Audit: Public Clouds

894. Is quality audit a prerequisite for program accreditation or program recognition?

895. What does an analysis of your organizations staff profile suggest in terms of its planning, and how is this being addressed?

896. Is the continuing professional education of key personnel account fored in detail?

897. How does your organization know that its staff embody the core knowledge, skills and characteristics for which it wishes to be recognized?

898. Are people allowed to contribute ideas?

899. How does your organization know that it is appropriately effective and constructive in preparing its staff for organizational aspirations?

900. How does your organization know that its relationship with its (past) staff is appropriately effective and constructive?

901. It is inappropriate to seek information about the Audit Panels preliminary views including questions like why do you ask that?

902. Are all complaints involving the possible failure of a device, labeling, or packaging to meet any of its specifications reviewed, evaluated, and investigated?

903. If your organization thinks it is doing something well, can it prove this?

904. What happens if your organization fails its Quality Audit?

905. How does your organization know that its system for ensuring that its training activities are appropriately resourced and support is appropriately effective and constructive?

906. Is there a written corporate quality policy?

907. How does your organization know that its system for inducting new staff to maximize workplace contributions are appropriately effective and constructive?

908. How does your organization know that its financial management system is appropriately effective and constructive?

909. Is your organizations resource allocation system properly aligned with its collection of intentions?

910. How does your organization know that its system for commercializing research outputs is appropriately effective and constructive?

911. Is progress against the intentions measurable?

912. How do you know what, specifically, is required of you in your work?

913. How does your organization know that its relationships with the community at large are

appropriately effective and constructive?

3.6 Team Directory: Public Clouds

914. Process decisions: is work progressing on schedule and per contract requirements?

915. When will you produce deliverables?

916. Process decisions: are all start-up, turn over and close out requirements of the contract satisfied?

917. How and in what format should information be presented?

918. When does information need to be distributed?

919. Timing: when do the effects of communication take place?

920. Contract requirements complied with?

921. Where will the product be used and/or delivered or built when appropriate?

922. Where should the information be distributed?

923. Who are your stakeholders (customers, sponsors, end users, team members)?

924. Who should receive information (all stakeholders)?

925. Have you decided when to celebrate the Public Clouds projects completion date?

926. Process decisions: are there any statutory or regulatory issues relevant to the timely execution of work?

927. Process decisions: do invoice amounts match accepted work in place?

928. Process decisions: how well was task order work performed?

929. Who will be the stakeholders on your next Public Clouds project?

930. Decisions: what could be done better to improve the quality of the constructed product?

931. Who are the Team Members?

932. Who will write the meeting minutes and distribute?

3.7 Team Operating Agreement: Public Clouds

933. What resources can be provided for the team in terms of equipment, space, time for training, protected time and space for meetings, and travel allowances?

934. What are the current caseload numbers in the unit?

935. Is compensation based on team and individual performance?

936. Do team members need to frequently communicate as a full group to make timely decisions?

937. How will group handle unplanned absences?

938. To whom do you deliver your services?

939. What are the safety issues/risks that need to be addressed and/or that the team needs to consider?

940. What is group supervision?

941. Did you determine the technology methods that best match the messages to be communicated?

942. Communication protocols: how will the team communicate?

943. Must your members collaborate successfully to complete Public Clouds projects?

944. Methodologies: how will key team processes be implemented, such as training, research, work deliverable production, review and approval processes, knowledge management, and meeting procedures?

945. Do you post meeting notes and the recording (if used) and notify participants?

946. Do you vary your voice pace, tone and pitch to engage participants and gain involvement?

947. Do you use a parking lot for any items that are important and outside of the agenda?

948. What is culture?

949. What are the boundaries (organizational or geographic) within which you operate?

950. Do you begin with a question to engage everyone?

951. Are there more than two functional areas represented by your team?

3.8 Team Performance Assessment: Public Clouds

952. How hard do you try to make a good selection?

953. Do you promptly inform members about major developments that may affect them?

954. To what degree are corresponding categories of skills either actually or potentially represented across the membership?

955. To what degree does the teams work approach provide opportunity for members to engage in fact-based problem solving?

956. To what degree do members articulate the goals beyond the team membership?

957. To what degree does the teams approach to its work allow for modification and improvement over time?

958. To what degree can the team ensure that all members are individually and jointly accountable for the teams purpose, goals, approach, and work-products?

959. To what degree is the team cognizant of small wins to be celebrated along the way?

960. Lack of method variance in self-reported affect and perceptions at work: Reality or artifact?

961. When a reviewer complains about method variance, what is the essence of the complaint?

962. If you have criticized someones work for method variance in your role as reviewer, what was the circumstance?

963. To what degree are staff involved as partners in the improvement process?

964. To what degree are the members clear on what they are individually responsible for and what they are jointly responsible for?

965. If you are worried about method variance before you collect data, what sort of design elements might you include to reduce or eliminate the threat of method variance?

966. How do you recognize and praise members for contributions?

967. Do friends perform better than acquaintances?

968. What do you think is the most constructive thing that could be done now to resolve considerations and disputes about method variance?

969. To what degree do team members feel that the purpose of the team is important, if not exciting?

970. How does Public Clouds project termination impact Public Clouds project team members?

971. How much interpersonal friction is there in your

team?

3.9 Team Member Performance Assessment: Public Clouds

972. Do the goals support your organizations goals?

973. Which training platform formats (i.e., mobile, virtual, videogame-based) were implemented in your effort(s)?

974. Does adaptive training work?

975. What are best practices in use for the performance measurement system?

976. What resources do you need?

977. How often are assessments to be conducted?

978. How do you use data to inform instruction and improve staff achievement?

979. Goals met?

980. How effective is training that is delivered through technology-based platforms?

981. How are training activities developed from a technical perspective?

982. How do you currently use the time that is available?

983. How will they be formed?

984. Who they are?

985. What instructional strategies were developed/ incorporated (e.g., direct instruction, indirect instruction, experiential learning, independent study, interactive instruction)?

986. To what degree can team members meet frequently enough to accomplish the teams ends?

987. What are top priorities?

988. For what period of time is a member rated?

989. What is collaboration?

990. How do you determine which data are the most important to use, analyze, or review?

3.10 Issue Log: Public Clouds

991. What date was the issue resolved?

992. Which team member will work with each stakeholder?

993. Why do you manage human resources?

994. What is the stakeholders political influence?

995. What help do you and your team need from the stakeholders?

996. Who do you turn to if you have questions?

997. How do you reply to this question; you am new here and managing this major program. How do you suggest you build your network?

998. Who reported the issue?

999. Are the Public Clouds project issues uniquely identified, including to which product they refer?

1000. Which stakeholders can influence others?

1001. What does the stakeholder need from the team?

1002. What effort will a change need?

1003. In classifying stakeholders, which approach to do so are you using?

1004. Is the issue log kept in a safe place?

1005. What is the impact on the risks?

4.0 Monitoring and Controlling Process Group: Public Clouds

1006. What is the expected monetary value of the Public Clouds project?

1007. Do clients benefit (change) from the services?

1008. What resources (both financial and non-financial) are available/needed?

1009. Where is the Risk in the Public Clouds project?

1010. What is the timeline?

1011. How well defined and documented were the Public Clouds project management processes you chose to use?

1012. Is the program making progress in helping to achieve the set results?

1013. Does the solution fit in with organizations technical architectural requirements?

1014. Is the program in place as intended?

1015. How can you make your needs known?

1016. User: who wants the information and what are they interested in?

1017. How can you monitor progress?

1018. How well did the chosen processes fit the needs of the Public Clouds project?

1019. How was the program set-up initiated?

1020. Is there adequate validation on required fields?

4.1 Project Performance Report: Public Clouds

1021. To what degree does the teams work approach provide opportunity for members to engage in open interaction?

1022. To what degree do team members frequently explore the teams purpose and its implications?

1023. To what degree are the demands of the task compatible with and converge with the mission and functions of the formal organization?

1024. To what degree does the formal organization make use of individual resources and meet individual needs?

1025. To what degree will new and supplemental skills be introduced as the need is recognized?

1026. To what degree can team members vigorously define the teams purpose in considerations with others who are not part of the functioning team?

1027. What is the degree to which rules govern information exchange between groups?

1028. To what degree does the teams work approach provide opportunity for members to engage in results-based evaluation?

1029. To what degree are the demands of the task

compatible with and converge with the relationships of the informal organization?

1030. To what degree are the skill areas critical to team performance present?

1031. To what degree are the tasks requirements reflected in the flow and storage of information?

1032. To what degree are fresh input and perspectives systematically caught and added (for example, through information and analysis, new members, and senior sponsors)?

1033. To what degree can the cognitive capacity of individuals accommodate the flow of information?

1034. To what degree can team members frequently and easily communicate with one another?

1035. To what degree do individual skills and abilities match task demands?

1036. To what degree are the goals realistic?

1037. What is the degree to which rules govern information exchange between individuals within your organization?

4.2 Variance Analysis: Public Clouds

1038. Are records maintained to show how management reserves are used?

1039. What business event causes fluctuations?

1040. How do you identify and isolate causes of favorable and unfavorable cost and schedule variances?

1041. Is the anticipated (firm and potential) business base Public Clouds projected in a rational, consistent manner?

1042. Do you identify potential or actual budget-based and time-based schedule variances?

1043. What can be the cause of an increase in costs?

1044. Favorable or unfavorable variance?

1045. Does the contractors system provide unit or lot costs when applicable?

1046. How do you verify authorization to proceed with all authorized work?

1047. Are data elements reconcilable between internal summary reports and reports forwarded to the stakeholders?

1048. What types of services and expense are shared between business segments?

1049. Does the contractors system identify work accomplishment against the schedule plan?

1050. What are the direct labor dollars and/or hours?

1051. What should management do?

1052. Who is generally responsible for monitoring and taking action on variances?

1053. How does your organization measure performance?

1054. Does the contractors system include procedures for measuring the performance of critical subcontractors?

1055. Who are responsible for overhead performance control of related costs?

1056. Are detailed work packages planned as far in advance as practicable?

4.3 Earned Value Status: Public Clouds

1057. How much is it going to cost by the finish?

1058. Where is evidence-based earned value in your organization reported?

1059. What is the unit of forecast value?

1060. If earned value management (EVM) is so good in determining the true status of a Public Clouds project and Public Clouds project its completion, why is it that hardly any one uses it in information systems related Public Clouds projects?

1061. Where are your problem areas?

1062. How does this compare with other Public Clouds projects?

1063. Verification is a process of ensuring that the developed system satisfies the stakeholders agreements and specifications; Are you building the product right? What do you verify?

1064. When is it going to finish?

1065. Earned value can be used in almost any Public Clouds project situation and in almost any Public Clouds project environment. it may be used on large Public Clouds projects, medium sized Public Clouds projects, tiny Public Clouds projects (in cut-down form), complex and simple Public Clouds projects and in any market sector. some people, of course, know all about earned value, they have used it for years - but perhaps not as effectively as they could have?

1066. Are you hitting your Public Clouds projects targets?

1067. Validation is a process of ensuring that the developed system will actually achieve the stakeholders desired outcomes; Are you building the right product? What do you validate?

4.4 Risk Audit: Public Clouds

1068. Level of preparation and skill?

1069. Are all managers or operators of the facility or equipment competent or qualified?

1070. Do you have financial policies and procedures in place to guide officers of your organization/treasurer/ general members?

1071. Does your board meet regularly and document all decisions and actions?

1072. Does your organization have or has considered the need for insurance covers: public liability, professional indemnity and directors and officers liability?

1073. What limitations do auditors face in effectively applying risk-assessment results to the risk of material misstatement measures?

1074. Estimated size of product in number of programs, files, transactions?

1075. What are the outcomes you are looking for?

1076. How do you prioritize risks?

1077. Does the Public Clouds project team have experience with the technology to be implemented?

1078. Is the technology to be built new to your

organization?

1079. Have permissions or required permits to use facilities managed by other parties been obtained?

1080. Has an event time line been developed?

1081. Do you record and file all audits?

1082. Has risk management been considered when planning an event?

1083. To what extent are auditors effective at linking business risks and management assertions?

1084. Do you promote education and training opportunities?

1085. How effective are your risk controls?

1086. Do you meet all obligations relating to funds secured from grants, loans and sponsors?

4.5 Contractor Status Report: Public Clouds

1087. If applicable; describe your standard schedule for new software version releases. Are new software version releases included in the standard maintenance plan?

1088. What is the average response time for answering a support call?

1089. What was the actual budget or estimated cost for your organizations services?

1090. Who can list a Public Clouds project as organization experience, your organization or a previous employee of your organization?

1091. What are the minimum and optimal bandwidth requirements for the proposed solution?

1092. How long have you been using the services?

1093. What was the final actual cost?

1094. Are there contractual transfer concerns?

1095. What process manages the contracts?

1096. What was the budget or estimated cost for your organizations services?

1097. How is risk transferred?

1098. What was the overall budget or estimated cost?

1099. Describe how often regular updates are made to the proposed solution. Are corresponding regular updates included in the standard maintenance plan?

4.6 Formal Acceptance: Public Clouds

1100. General estimate of the costs and times to complete the Public Clouds project?

1101. Did the Public Clouds project achieve its MOV?

1102. Does it do what Public Clouds project team said it would?

1103. Was the Public Clouds project managed well?

1104. Was business value realized?

1105. Was the Public Clouds project goal achieved?

1106. How does your team plan to obtain formal acceptance on your Public Clouds project?

1107. Do you buy-in installation services?

1108. Was the client satisfied with the Public Clouds project results?

1109. Who would use it?

1110. How well did the team follow the methodology?

1111. What is the Acceptance Management Process?

1112. Is formal acceptance of the Public Clouds project product documented and distributed?

1113. What features, practices, and processes proved

to be strengths or weaknesses?

1114. Does it do what client said it would?

1115. What was done right?

1116. Have all comments been addressed?

1117. What are the requirements against which to test, Who will execute?

1118. Do you buy pre-configured systems or build your own configuration?

1119. Did the Public Clouds project manager and team act in a professional and ethical manner?

5.0 Closing Process Group: Public Clouds

1120. What was learned?

1121. What is the risk of failure to your organization?

1122. What areas were overlooked on this Public Clouds project?

1123. Mitigate. what will you do to minimize the impact should a risk event occur?

1124. What is an Encumbrance?

1125. Is there a clear cause and effect between the activity and the lesson learned?

1126. Were risks identified and mitigated?

1127. What were things that you did very well and want to do the same again on the next Public Clouds project?

1128. Can the lesson learned be replicated?

1129. What is the Public Clouds project Management Process?

1130. What is the Public Clouds project name and date of completion?

1131. What were the actual outcomes?

1132. When will the Public Clouds project be done?

1133. What business situation is being addressed?

1134. How well did you do?

1135. What can you do better next time, and what specific actions can you take to improve?

1136. Did the delivered product meet the specified requirements and goals of the Public Clouds project?

5.1 Procurement Audit: Public Clouds

1137. Access to data, including standing data, and the identification of restriction levels and authorised personnel was in place?

1138. Does the individual approving disbursements sign or initial the document?

1139. Are information gathered to produce knowledge about procured goods and services, prices paid and supplier performance?

1140. Is there a formal program of inservice training for personnel in the business management function?

1141. Are proper financing arrangements taken?

1142. Budget controls: does your organization maintain an up-to-date (approved) budget for all funded activities, and perform a comparison of that budget with actual expenditures for each budget category?

1143. Is there a purchasing policy as to the amount of an order on which bidding is required?

1144. Does the procurement function/unit have the ability to apply public procurement principles and to prepare tender and contract documents?

1145. Which are main risks and controls of each phase?

1146. Was the tender clearly and properly specified, including evaluation criteria and knowing about the market and therefore not over-prescriptive and receptive to innovation?

1147. Is the procurement process fully digitalized?

1148. Did your organization decide upon an adequate and admissible procurement procedure?

1149. Has the award included no items different from the already stated contained in bid specifications?

1150. When corresponding references were made, was a precise description of the performance not otherwise possible and were the already stated references accompanied by the words or equivalent?

1151. Are purchase orders pre-numbered?

1152. Is your organization aware and informed about international procurement standards and good practice?

1153. Is there an effective risk management system continuously monitoring procurement risk?

1154. Are risks in the external environment identified, for example: Budgetary constraints?

1155. Are there mechanisms in place to evaluate the performance of the departments suppliers?

1156. Were additional works charged at the unit prices agreed in the initial contract?

5.2 Contract Close-Out: Public Clouds

1157. Have all contracts been completed?

1158. Was the contract complete without requiring numerous changes and revisions?

1159. Parties: who is involved?

1160. Have all contracts been closed?

1161. Was the contract sufficiently clear so as not to result in numerous disputes and misunderstandings?

1162. What is capture management?

1163. Has each contract been audited to verify acceptance and delivery?

1164. Have all contract records been included in the Public Clouds project archives?

1165. Change in knowledge?

1166. Are the signers the authorized officials?

1167. How is the contracting office notified of the automatic contract close-out?

1168. Have all acceptance criteria been met prior to final payment to contractors?

1169. Why Outsource?

1170. Change in attitude or behavior?

1171. Parties: Authorized?

1172. How does it work?

1173. Was the contract type appropriate?

1174. Change in circumstances?

1175. What happens to the recipient of services?

1176. How/when used ?

5.3 Project or Phase Close-Out: Public Clouds

1177. Who exerted influence that has positively affected or negatively impacted the Public Clouds project?

1178. What stakeholder group needs, expectations, and interests are being met by the Public Clouds project?

1179. What are the marketing communication needs for each stakeholder?

1180. How often did each stakeholder need an update?

1181. What are the mandatory communication needs for each stakeholder?

1182. Did the delivered product meet the specified requirements and goals of the Public Clouds project?

1183. Was the schedule met?

1184. What is a Risk?

1185. What are the informational communication needs for each stakeholder?

1186. What is in it for you?

1187. Did the Public Clouds project management

methodology work?

1188. What process was planned for managing issues/ risks?

1189. What is this stakeholder expecting?

1190. In addition to assessing whether the Public Clouds project was successful, it is equally critical to analyze why it was or was not fully successful. Are you including this?

1191. Who controlled the resources for the Public Clouds project?

1192. Which changes might a stakeholder be required to make as a result of the Public Clouds project?

1193. What could have been improved?

5.4 Lessons Learned: Public Clouds

1194. Did the Public Clouds project improve the team members reputations, skills, personal development?

1195. What is below the surface?

1196. What on the Public Clouds project worked well and was effective in the delivery of the product?

1197. Did the delivered product meet the specified requirements and goals of the Public Clouds project?

1198. How well were Public Clouds project issues communicated throughout your involvement in the Public Clouds project?

1199. Will the information remain current?

1200. What were the key issues?

1201. Does the lesson describe a function that would be done differently the next time?

1202. What was the methodology behind successful learning experiences, and how might they be applied to the broader challenge of your organizations knowledge management?

1203. What is (are) the indicator(s) of success?

1204. How was the political and social history changed over the life of the Public Clouds project?

1205. What is your working hypothesis, if you have one?

1206. What were the challenges and pitfalls?

1207. What are the skills directly related to the task?

1208. What solutions or recommendations can you offer that would have improved some aspect of the Public Clouds project?

1209. What worked well/did not work well?

1210. What were the most significant issues on this Public Clouds project?

1211. What are the funding priorities for intelligence?

1212. Where could you improve?

1213. What if anything has been lacking?

Index

custom22
customer   22, 28, 32, 37, 40, 75, 88, 91, 105, 108, 111, 116,
119, 126, 140, 177, 193, 197-200
customers   1, 21, 26, 28, 45, 53, 55, 60, 63, 69, 87, 103, 105,
109, 111, 113, 115, 117, 119, 126, 143, 180, 201, 214, 224
customize   210
cut-down   241
damage   1, 197
Dashboard   8
dashboards   88
day-to-day   91, 99
deadlines   22, 121
dealing   21
debriefing   205
deceitful   100
decide 79, 252
decided   84, 224
deciding   105
decision   5, 45, 57, 77-78, 81, 84, 196, 211-212, 219-220
decisions   74, 78-79, 81-82, 84, 89, 95, 124, 185-186, 219,
224-226, 243
decomposed 166
decrease   181
dedicate   185
dedicated   7
deeper   10
defect 136, 181
defective   193
defects   124, 181, 215
define 2, 26, 40, 62, 68, 74, 148, 167, 181, 188, 220, 237
defined   10, 15, 21, 26-27, 29-31, 33-35, 37-38, 42, 56, 61,
70, 72, 87, 99, 143, 152, 156, 165, 169, 171-172, 180, 182, 188,
190, 207, 235
defines 23, 33-34, 163-164
defining   7, 110, 127, 145
definite   95, 156
definition   18, 27, 31-32, 34-35, 152, 177, 184
degree   200, 228-229, 232, 237-238
delayed   158
delaying   48
delays 52, 167, 170
delegated   34
deletions   88

negative   108, 169
negatively   255
negotiate   100
negotiated   106
neither 1
network   3, 160, 233
Neutral 10, 15, 26, 42, 56, 72, 87, 99
normal 89
Notice 1
noticing   219
notified   206, 253
notify   227
number   25, 41, 44, 55, 71, 86, 98, 122, 156, 163, 181, 243,
259
numbers   101, 226
numerous   253
objection   17, 19
objective   7, 52, 186, 190, 220
objectives   17, 22-23, 26, 30, 40, 67, 91, 98, 103, 110, 115,
119, 124, 139, 170, 177, 189, 195, 201, 208, 214
observe   187
observed   79
observing   146
obsolete   101
obstacles   24, 158, 167, 175
obtain 105, 247
obtained   28, 152, 244
obtaining   46
obviously   10
occurred   166, 180
occurrence   215
occurring   77, 125, 195
occurs 43, 93, 132, 200, 212
offerings   60, 76
offerors 206
office   214, 253
officer 205
officers 243
officials 253
offshore   139
one-time   7
ongoing   82, 93, 155, 167
On-premise   118

CPSIA information can be obtained
at www.ICGtesting.com
Printed in the USA
BVHW082017110819
555624BV00016BA/2001/P

9 780655 833536